ESTATE PUB   S

CORNWALL

Street maps with index
Administrative Districts
Population Gazetteer
Road Map with index
Postcodes

COUNTY RED BOOKS

This atlas is intended for those requiring street maps of the historical and commercial centres of towns within the county. Each locality is normally presented on one or two pages and although, with many small towns, this space is sufficient to portray the whole urban area, the maps of large towns and cities are for centres only and are not intended to be comprehensive. Such coverage in Super and Local Red Books (see page 2).

Every effort has been made to verify the accuracy of information in this book but the publishers cannot accept responsibility for expense or loss caused by any error or omission. Information that will be of assistance to the user of these maps will be welcomed.

The representation of a road, track or footpath on the maps in this atlas is no evidence of the existence of a right of way.

Street plans prepared and published by ESTATE PUBLICATIONS, Bridewell House, TENTERDEN, KENT.
The Publishers acknowledge the co-operation of the local authorities
of towns represented in this atlas.

Ordnance Survey® This product includes mapping data licensed from Ordnance Survey®
with the permission of the Controller of Her Majesty's Stationery Office.

COUNTY RED BOOK

CORNWALL

contains street maps for each town centre

SUPER & LOCAL RED BOOKS

are street atlases with comprehensive local coverage

TRURO & FALMOUTH

including: Carnon Downs, Mylor Bridge, Penryn, Perranwell, St. Mawes, Threemilestone etc.

ST. IVES & PENZANCE

including: Carbis Bay, Copperhouse, Hayle, Lelant, Marazion, St. Just etc.

CONTENTS

LEGEND TO STREET MAPS

One-Way Street	→	Post Office	●
Pedestrianized	▨	Public Convenience	⒞
Car Park	Ⓟ	Place of Worship	+

Scale of street plans: 4 Inches to 1 mile (unless otherwise stated on the map).

ND POINT

E · Hartland · Clovelly

Woolfardisworthy

Bideford · Newton Tracey

South Molton

Chittlehampton

Dulverton

· Morebath

Buckland Brewer

Great Torrington

· Roborough

King's Nympton

Meshaw

Oakford

Bampton

Rackenford

Bredworthy

Stibb Cross

Merton · Dolton

Chulmleigh

Witheridge

Sampford Peverell

Kilkhampton

Shebbear · Petrockstow

Worlington

Tiverton

Chawleigh

· Stratton

Sheepwash

Winkleigh

Lapford

Cheriton Fitzpaine

Morchard Bishop

· Bickleigh Bradninch

Marhamchurch

Holsworthy

Hatherleigh

Highampton

North Tawton

Exbourne

Copplestone

Silverton

Poundstock

Halwill

· Northlew

Bow

Thorverton

Crediton

Week St. Mary

Yeoford

Broad Clyst

Ashwater

Okehampton

Spreyton

Whitestone

Rockb...

Boyton

Bratton Clovelly

D E V O N

Yes Tor

South Zeal

Tedburn St. Mary

Bridestowe

Dunsford

EXETER

Cornwall Egloskerry

High Willhays

Chagford

Topsham

Launceston

Lifton

Lewtrenchard N. Brenton

Lydford

Cut Hill

Moretonhampstead

Chillaton

D A R T M O O R

· Lewannick

North Hill

Milton Abbot

Mary Tavy

Chudleigh

Starcross

MIN

Great Mis Tor

Two Bridges

Widecombe in the Moor

Bovey Tracey

· Ideford

Dawlish

OR

Caradon Hill

Tavistock

Princetown

Bickington

Teignmouth

St. ...eot

Pensilva · Callington

Gunnislake

Horrabridge

Ryder's Hill

Ashburton

Newton Abbot

Kingskerswell

· Yelverton

· **Liskeard**

Bere Alston

Bere Ferrers

Buckfastleigh

Torquay

Caradon

Tamerton Foliot

South Brent

Totnes

TORBAY

Paignton

Lanreath

St.Germans

Saltash

PLYMOUTH

Dittisham

Berry Head

Brixham

W. Looe

Sandplace

Torpoint

· Plympton

Ivybridge

Halwell

Kingswear

Polperro

E. Looe

St. George's or Looe I.

Millbrook

Brixton

Yealmpton

· Modbury

Dartmouth

Mew Stone

Rame

Rame Head

ROSCOFF ST. MALO

Newton Ferrers

Kingston

Slapton

Stoke Fleming

Stoke Pt.

Kingsbridge

Torcross

Thurlestone

Bolt Tail

Salcombe

START POINT

Bolt Head

Prawle Pt.

Eddystone

—— County boundary

—— District boundary

0   10 miles

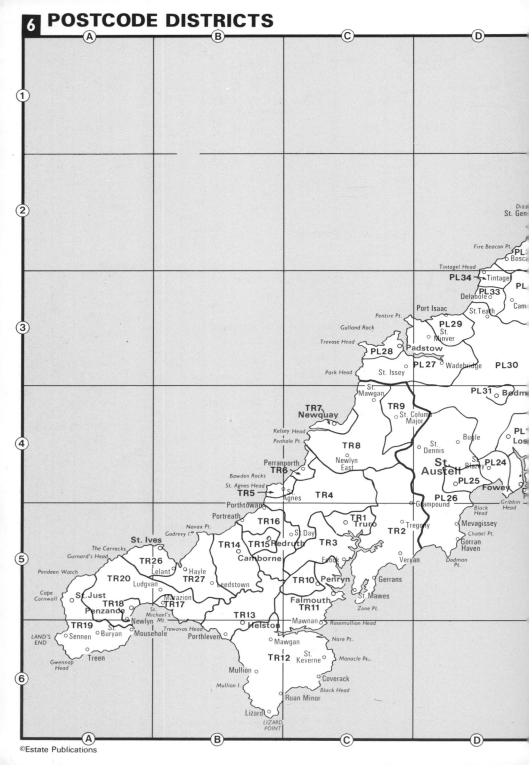

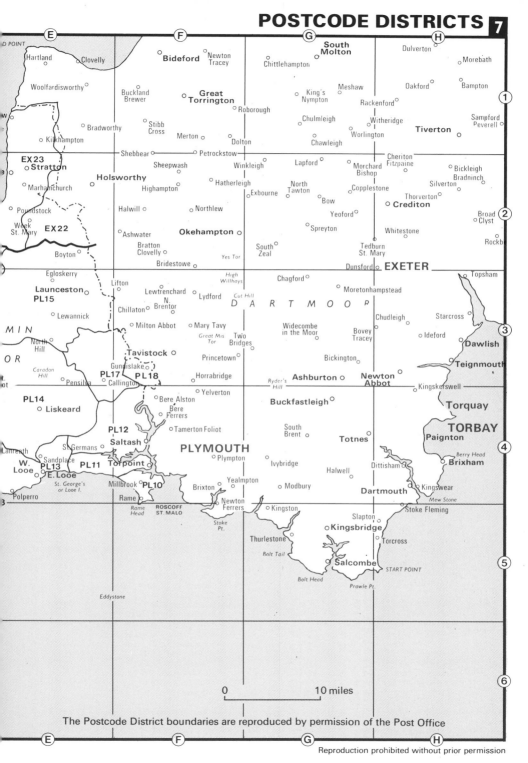

E   F   G   H

D POINT
Hartland   Clovelly
Woolfardisworthy
Bideford   Newton Tracey
     Chittlehampton
South Molton
Dulverton   Morebath

Buckland Brewer
Great Torrington
Roborough
King's Nympton   Meshaw
Oakford   Bampton
①

Bradworthy   Stibb Cross
Merton
Chulmleigh
Rackenford
Witheridge
Tiverton
Sampford Peverell

Kilkhampton
Dolton
Chawleigh
Worlington

EX23 Stratton
Shebbear   Petrockstow
Cheriton Fitzpaine
Bickleigh
Bradninch
②

Holsworthy
Sheepwash   Winkleigh
Lapford
Morchard Bishop
Silverton

Marhamchurch
Highampton   Hatherleigh
North Tawton
Copplestone
Thorverton

Poundstock
Halwill   Northlew
Exbourne
Bow
Crediton
Broad Clyst

Week St. Mary   **EX22**
Ashwater
Okehampton
Yeoford
Whitestone
Rockb

Boyton   Bratton Clovelly
South Zeal
Spreyton
Tedburn St. Mary
②

Bridestowe   Yes Tor
Dunsford
EXETER

Egloskerry
High Willhays
Chagford
Topsham

Launceston PL15   Lifton
Lewtrenchard   Lydford
Cut Hill
Moretonhampstead

Lewannick   Chillaton   N. Brentor
D A R T M O O R
Chudleigh
Starcross
③

MIN   North Hill
Milton Abbot   Mary Tavy
Great Mis Tor   Two Bridges
Widecombe in the Moor
Bovey Tracey
Ideford
Dawlish

OR   Caradon Hill
Tavistock
Princetown
Bickington
Teignmouth

Pensilva   Gunnislake **PL17 PL18**
Horrabridge
Ryder's Hill
Ashburton
Newton Abbot
Kingskerswell

PL14
Callington
Yelverton
Buckfastleigh
Torquay

Liskeard
Bere Alston   Bere Ferrers
South Brent
TORBAY
Tamerton Foliot
Paignton
④

PL12
Saltash
PLYMOUTH
Totnes
Berry Head
Brixham

Lanreath   St.Germans
Plympton
Ivybridge
Halwell
Dittisham

W. Looe   Sandplace **PL11**
Torpoint
Yealmpton
Kingswear

PL13 E. Looe
Millbrook **PL10**
Brixton   Modbury
Dartmouth
Mew Stone

Polperro   St. George's or Looe I.
Rame
Newton Ferrers
Kingston
Stoke Fleming

Rame Head   **ROSCOFF ST. MALO**
Stoke Pt.
Slapton
START POINT
⑤

Thurlestone   **Kingsbridge**
Torcross

Bolt Tail   **Salcombe**

Eddystone
Bolt Head   Prawle Pt.
⑥

0   10 miles

E   F   G   H

GAZETTEER INDEX TO ROAD MAP
with populations

County of Cornwall population **466,377**

Newlyn		10 A5
Newlyn East **1,377**		10 C4
Newquay **17,390**		10 C4
North Hill **837**		11 E3
North Petherwin **658**		*
North Tamerton **276**		*
Otterham **208**		*
Padstow **2,855**		10 C3
Paul **229**		*
Pelynt **1,079**		11 E4
Penryn **5,864**		10 C5
Pensilva		11 E3
Penzance **20,284**		10 A5
Perranaworthal **1,495**		10 C5
Perranporth		10 C4
Perranuthnoe **1,832**		10 B5
Perranzabuloe **5,220**		*
Philleigh **166**		*
Pillaton **485**		*
Polperro		11 E4
Polruan		10 D4
Porthleven **3,123**		10 B6
Porthtowan		10 B5
Port Isaac		10 D3
Portreath **1,251**		10 B5
Poundstock **789**		11 E2
Probus **1,827**		10 C5
Quethiock **422**		*
Rame (Maker-wth-Rame) **1,040**		11 F4
Redruth **12,111**		10 B5
Roche **2,344**		10 D4
Ruanlaniherne **264**		*
Ruan Minor		10 C6
St. Agnes **6,592**		10 C4
St. Allen **374**		*
St. Anthony-in-Meneage **192**		*
St. Austell **20,267**		10 D4
St. Blazey **6,121**		10 D4
St. Breock **700**		*
St. Breward **800**		*
St. Buryan **1,157**		10 A6
St. Cleer **3,087**		11 E4
St. Clement **1,150**		*
St. Clether **154**		*
St. Columb Major **3,144**		10 C4
St. Day **1,750**		10 C5
St. Dennis **2,249**		10 D4
St. Dominick **841**		*
St. Endellion **1,100**		*
St. Enoder **2,977**		10 C4
St. Erme **1,189**		*
St. Erth **1,220**		*
St. Ervan **478**		*
St. Eval **1,168**		*
St. Ewe **426**		*
St. Gennys **807**		10 D2
St. Germans **2,463**		11 E4
St. Gluvias **1,227**		*
St. Goran **1,306**		*
St. Hilary **707**		*
St. Issey **762**		10 C3
St. Ive **2,102**		11 E4
St. Ives **10,964**		10 B5
St. John **324**		*
St. Juliot **288**		*
St. Just **4,424**		10 A5
St. Just in Roseland **1,172**		*
St. Keverne **1,843**		10 C6
St. Kew **933**		*
St. Keyne **450**		*
St. Levan **517**		*
St. Mabyn **589**		*
St. Martin **516**		*
St. Marin-in-Meneage **306**		*
St. Mawes		10 C5
St. Mellion **248**		*
St. Merryn **1,395**		10 C3
St. Mewan **2,954**		10 D4
St. Michael Caerhays **77**		*
St. Michael Penkevil **206**		*
St. Michael's Mount **36**		10 B5
St. Minver Highlands & Lowlands **2,194**		10 D3
St. Neot **891**		11 E3
St. Pinnock **454**		*
St. Sampson **253**		*
St. Stephen-in-Brannel **5,490**		10 C4
St. Stephens (by Launceston) **330**		*
St. Teath **2,070**		10 D3
St. Thomas the Apostle **813**		*
St. Tudy **565**		*
St. Veep **322**		*
St. Wenn **313**		*
St. Winnow **286**		*
Saltash **14,139**		11 F4
Sancreed **653**		*
Sandplace		11 E4
Sennen **842**		10 A6
Sheviock **796**		*
Sithney **705**		10 B5
South Hill **483**		*
South Petherwin **867**		11 E3
Stithians **2,039**		10 C5
Stoke Climsland **1,466**		11 E3
Stratton (with Bude) **8,071**		11 E2
Tintagel **1,721**		10 D3
Torpoint **8,238**		11 F4
Towednack **324**		*
Treen		10 A6
Tregony **729**		10 C5
Tremaine **84**		*
Treneglos **112**		*
Tresmeer **176**		*
Trevalga **86**		*
Treverbyn **5,443**		*
Trewen **124**		*
Truro **16,522**		10 C5
Tywardreath **3,114**		*
Veryan **877**		10 C5
Wadebridge **5,291**		10 D3
Warbstow **410**		*
Warleggan **203**		*
Week St. Mary **527**		11 E2
Wendron **2,434**		10 B5
Werrington **440**		*
West Looe (with E. Looe) **5,265**		11 E4
Whitstone **430**		*
Withiel **339**		*
Zennor **242**		10 A5

Population figures are based upon the 1991 census and relate to the local authority area or parish as constituted at that date. Places with no population figure form part of a larger local authority area or parish. District boundaries are shown on pages 4-5.
Population figures in bold type.   *Parish not shown on map pages 10-11 due to limitation of scale.

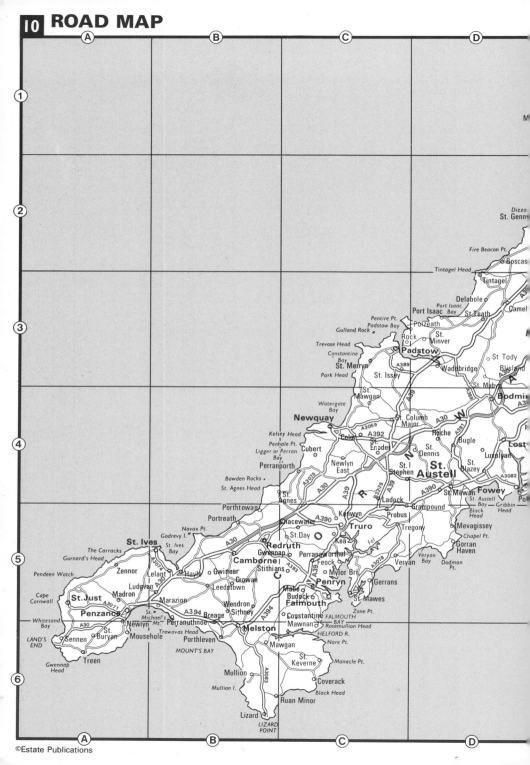

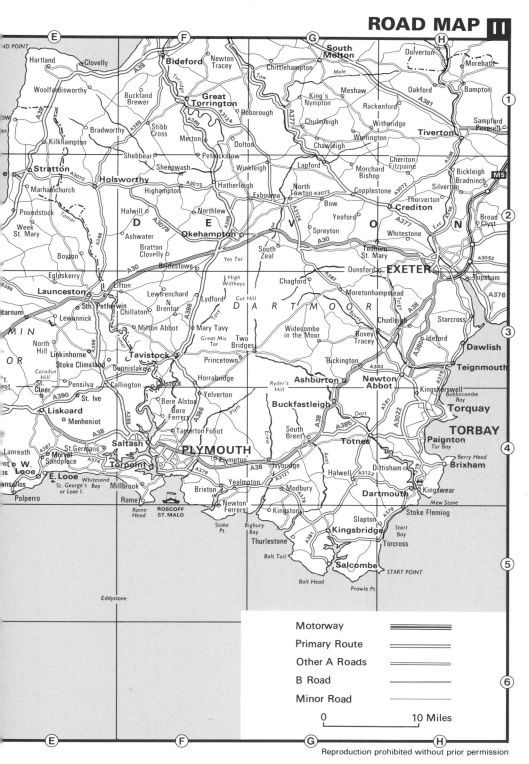

ROAD MAP **II**

Legend

Motorway
Primary Route
Other A Roads
B Road
Minor Road

0   10 Miles

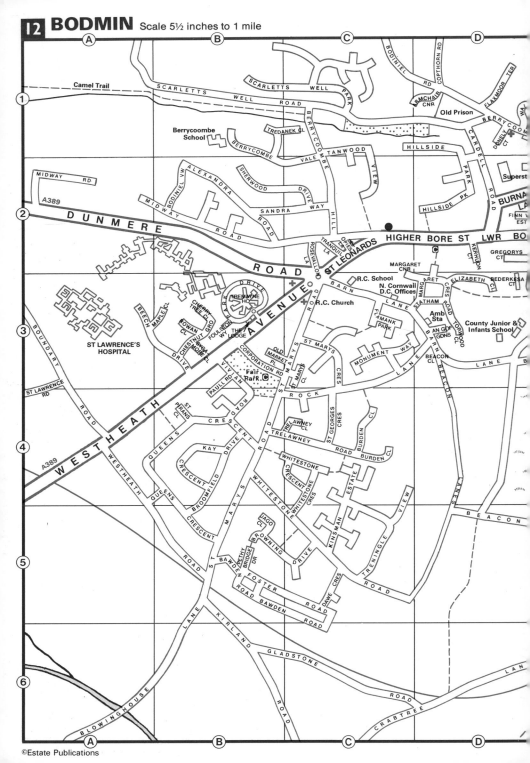

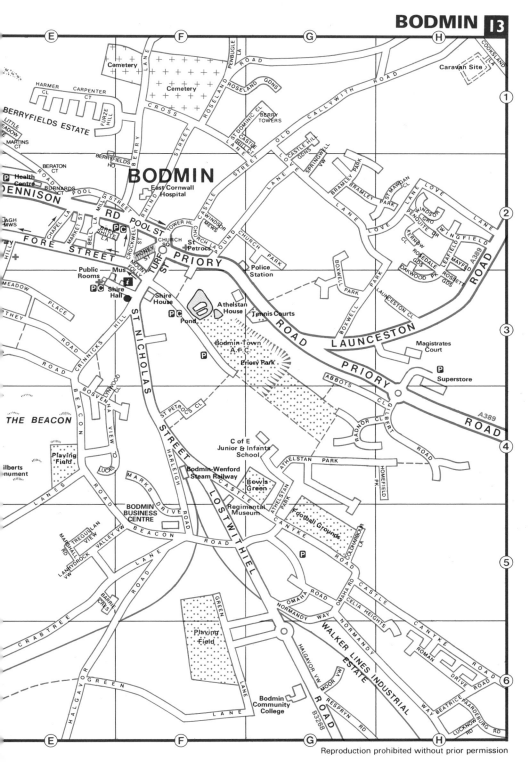

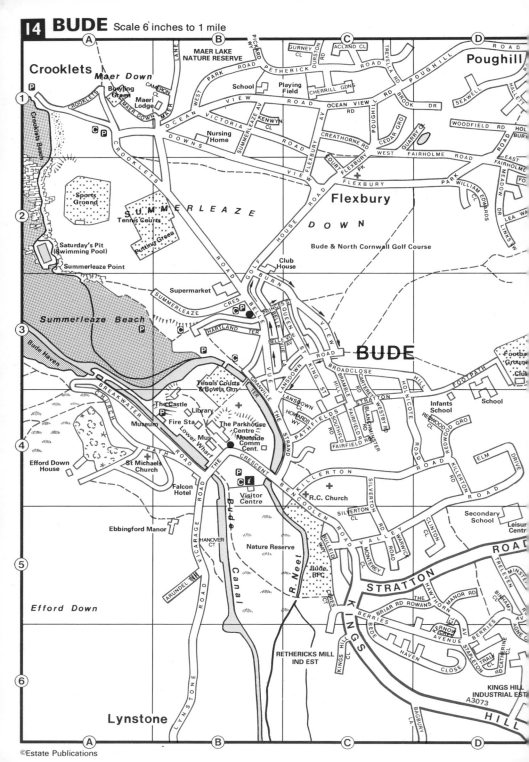

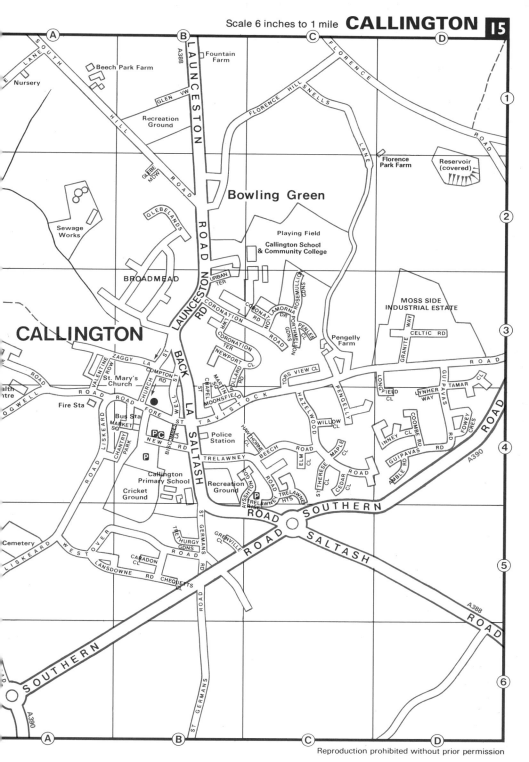

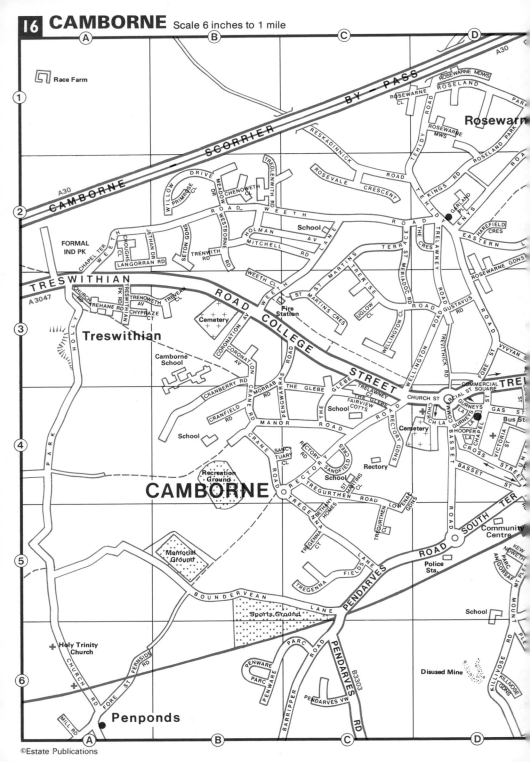

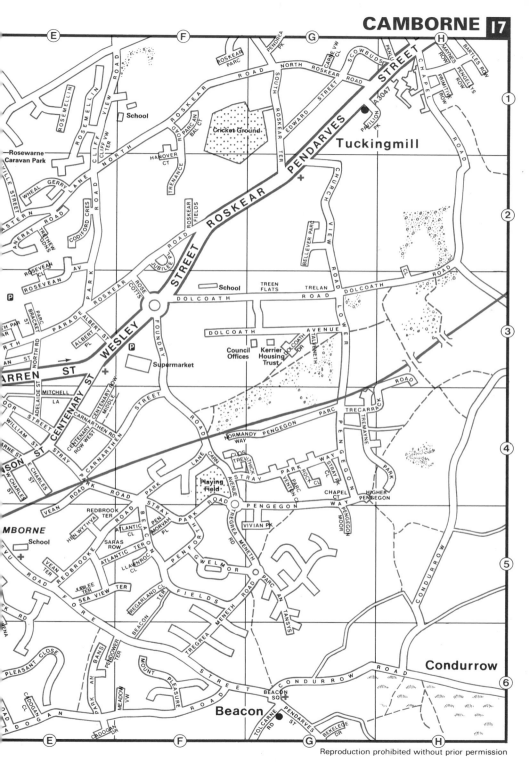

CAMBORNE 17

Tuckingmill

Condurrow

Beacon

MBORNE

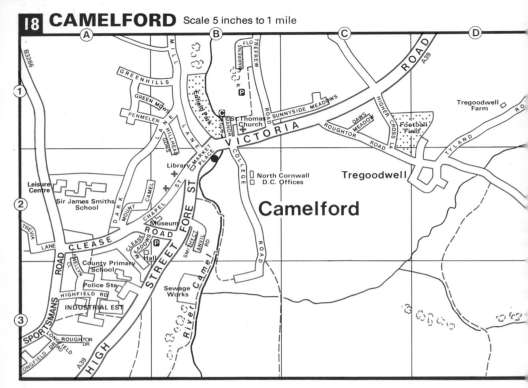

Camelford

Tregoodwell

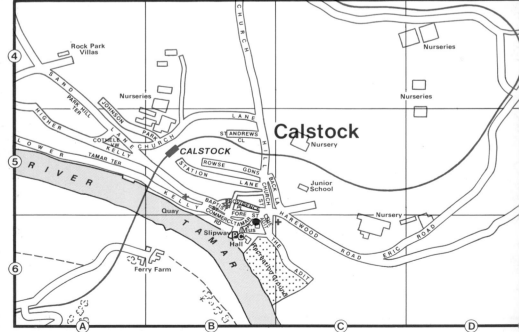

Calstock

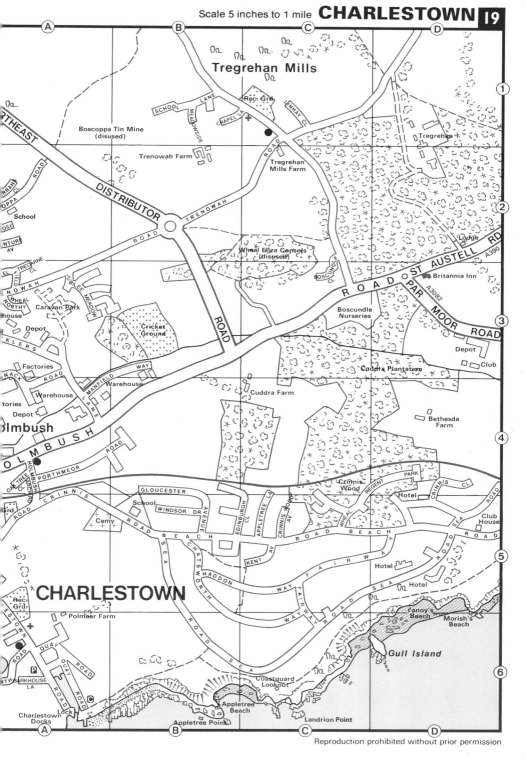

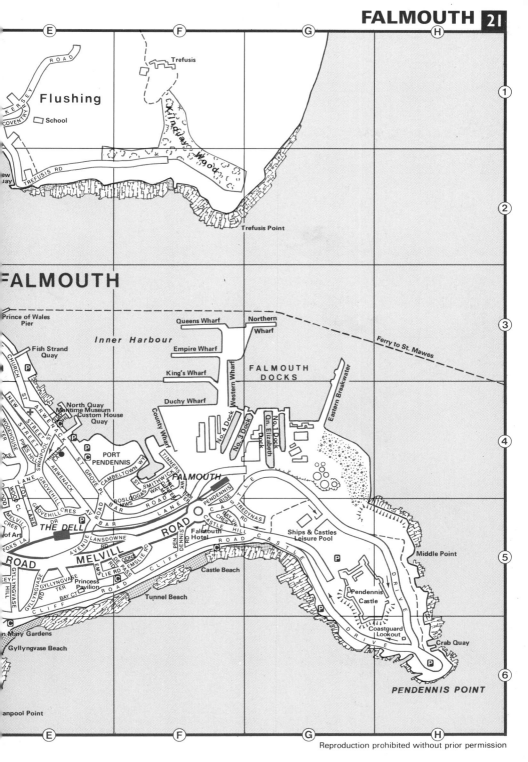

Flushing

Trefusis

School

ROAD

COVENTRY KEY

TREFUSIS RD

Kilndways Wood

Trefusis Point

FALMOUTH

Prince of Wales
Pier

Inner Harbour

Queens Wharf

Northern
Wharf

Ferry to St. Mawes

Fish Strand
Quay

Empire Wharf

FALMOUTH
DOCKS

King's Wharf

Duchy Wharf

Eastern Breakwater

North Quay
Maritime Museum
Custom House
Quay

Western Wharf

No. 4 Dock

No. 3 Dock

Qn. Elizabeth
Dock

No. 1 Dock

CHURCH

NEW STREET

ARWENACK ST

WOODHOUSE TER

PINES WILLIAMS
QDS

GROVE PL

ST GROVE PL

County Wharf

PORT
PENDENNIS

TINNERS

CAMBELTOWN WY

SMITHWICK
WAY

FALMOUTH

GROVEHILL CRES

ROSLOGGAS WAY

BAR ROAD

PENDENNIS RISE

CASTLE RISE

BAY VIEW CRES

REDYNAS RD

FOX CL

GROVEHILL CRES

THE DELL

Art

AVENUE

LANSDOWNE
RD

PENDENNIS RD

CASTLE HILL

Ships & Castles
Leisure Pool

Middle Point

MELVILL

ROAD

Falmouth
Hotel

ROAD

CASTLE

DRIVE

FOXS LA

GYLLYNGVASE
HILL

EMSLIE RD

PEMSLIE RD

GDNS

CLIFF ROAD

Castle Beach

P

Pendennis
Castle

GYLLYNGVASE RD

GYLLYNGVASE
TER

BAY CT

Princess
Pavilion

Tunnel Beach

DRIVE

Coastguard
Lookout

Crab Quay

ROAD

CLIFF

Mary Gardens

Gyllyngvase Beach

anpool Point

PENDENNIS POINT

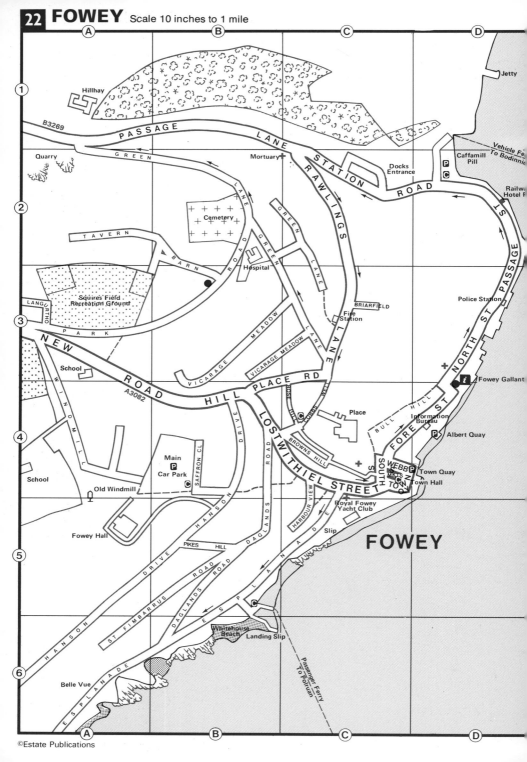

Hillhay

B3269

PASSAGE

GREEN

Quarry

Mortuary

STATION

RAWLINGS

Docks Entrance

ROAD

LANE

GREEN LANE

Cemetery

TAVERN

BARN

Vehicle Fe... To Bodinnie

Caffamill Pill

Railwa... Hotel

P C

ROAD

LANGURTHO

PARK

NEW

Squires' Field Recreation Ground

Hospital

VICARAGE MEADOW LANE

ROAD

GREEN LANE

BRIARFIELD

Fire Station

Police Station

NORTH ST PASSAGE

School

ROAD

A3082

HILL

PLACE RD

VICARAGE MEADOW

LANE

FORE ST

BULL HILL

Fowey Gallant

WINDMILL

School

Old Windmill

Main Car Park

P

C

SAFFRON CL.

DRIVE

HANSON ROAD

LOSTWITHIEL STREET

BROWNS HILL

Place

Information Bureau

P

Albert Quay

WEBB

MKS

Town Quay

SOUTH TOWN

Town Hall

Fowey Hall

PIKES HILL

DAGLANDS ROAD

HARBOUR VIEW

Royal Fowey Yacht Club

Slip

FOWEY

DRIVE

HANSON

ST FIMBARRUS ROAD

DAGLANDS ROAD

ESPLANADE

Whitehouse Beach

Landing Slip

C

Passenger Ferry To Polruan

Belle Vue

©Estate Publications

Jetty

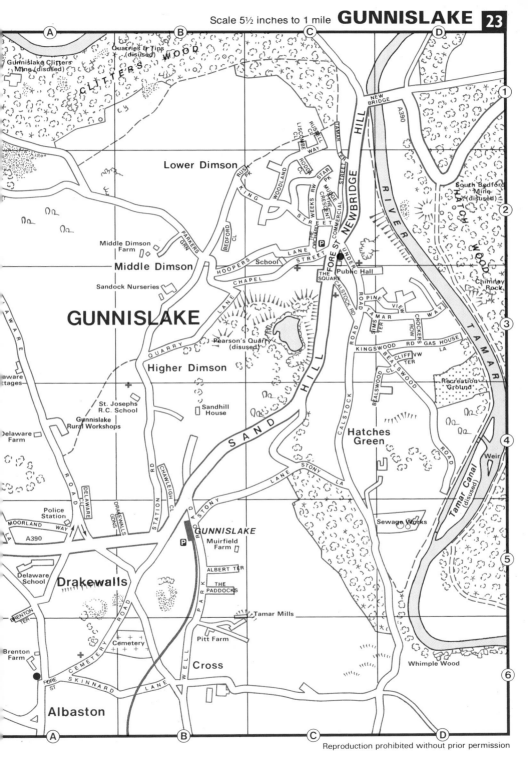

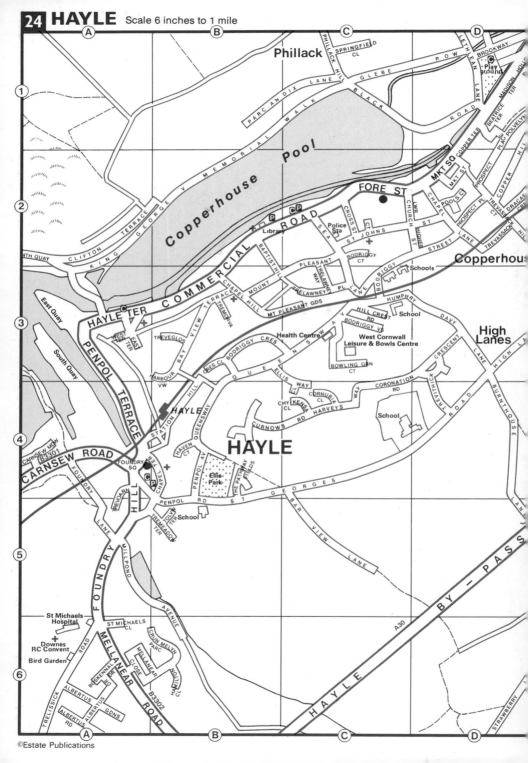

24 HAYLE Scale 6 inches to 1 mile

Phillack

Copperhouse Pool

FORE ST

Copperhou

High Lanes

HAYLE

HAYLE

Ellis Park

St Michaels Hospital

Downes RC Convent

Bird Garden

BY-PASS

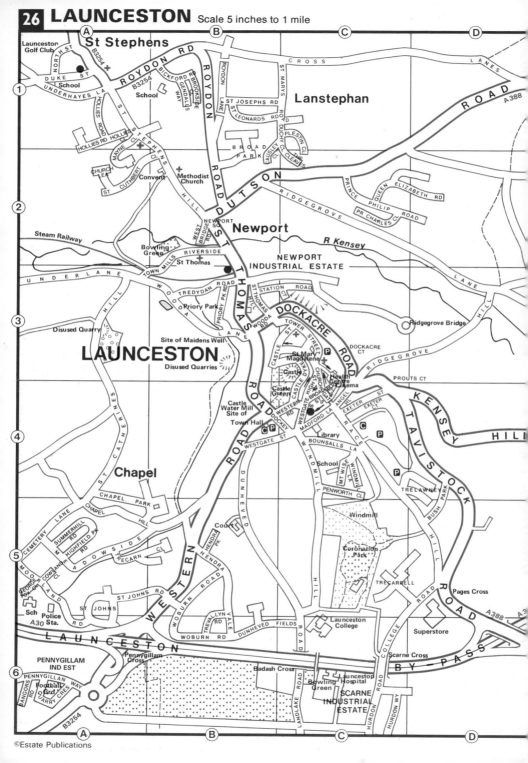

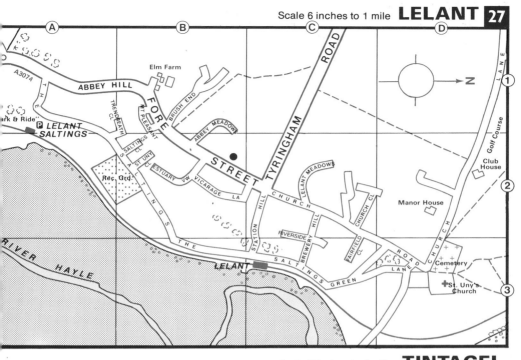

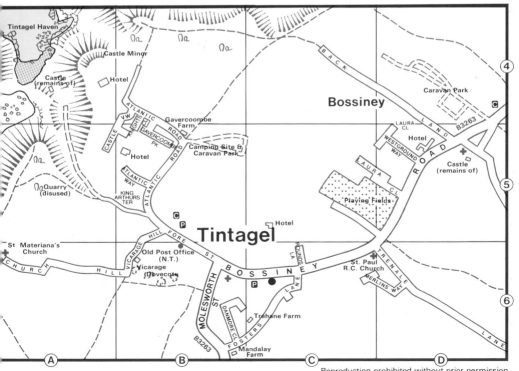

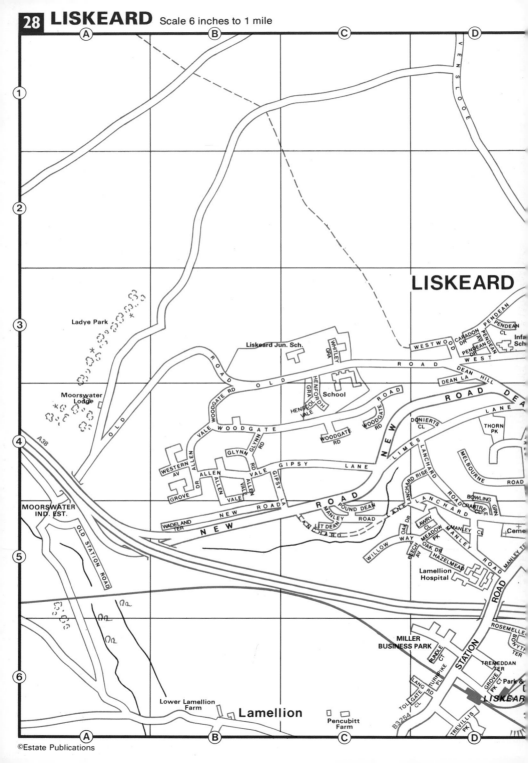

LISKEARD

Ladye Park

Liskeard Jun. Sch.

Moorswater Lodge

WESTWOOD ROAD

PENDEAN DR
CANADON DR
PENDEAN
PENDEAN CL
PENDEAN TER
WEST
Infa Sch

DEAN LA
DEAN HILL
ROAD DEA

WHITLEY GRA

HENFORD GRA
HENSCOL VALE
School

OLD ROAD

WOODGATE RD
WOODGATE

WOODGATE RD
WOODGATE RD

LANE
THORN PK

MELBOURNE ROAD

NEW ROAD
LIMES

DONIERTS CL

VALE ALLEN DR

WESTERN AV
ALLEN GROVE DR
GLYNN RD
ALLEN VALE
GLYNN RD VALE
ALLEN VALE

GIPSY LANE
GIPSY VALE

LANCHARD

LANCHARD RISE
LANCHARD
LANCHARD RD
CRABTRE

BOWLING GRN
CemE

A38

MOORSWATER IND. EST.

OLD STATION ROAD

WADELAND TER
NEW ROAD
NEW ROAD

POUND DEAN
MANLEY
LIT DEAN
ROAD
ROAD

OAK DR
WILLOW WAY
BEECH AV
AWRY
MEADOW PK
OAK DR
HAZELMEAD

MANLEY CL
MANLEY RD
MANLEY TE

Lamellion Hospital

ROSEMELLE
BOVYTH
TER

MILLER BUSINESS PARK

RUNDLE CT

LANG RD
TOLLGATE CL
TURNPIKE

B3254

STATION ROAD

TREMEDDAN TER
GROVE CT
Park &

LISKEAR

TREVILLIS PK

Lower Lamellion Farm

Lamellion

Pencubitt Farm

VENSLOOE

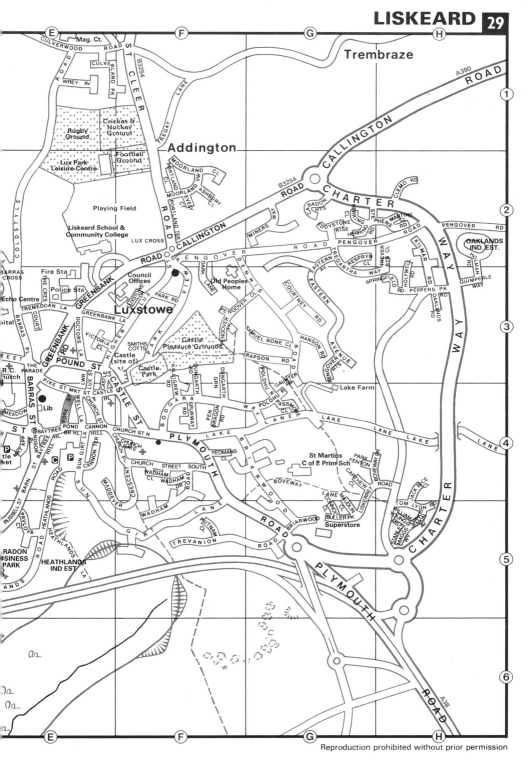

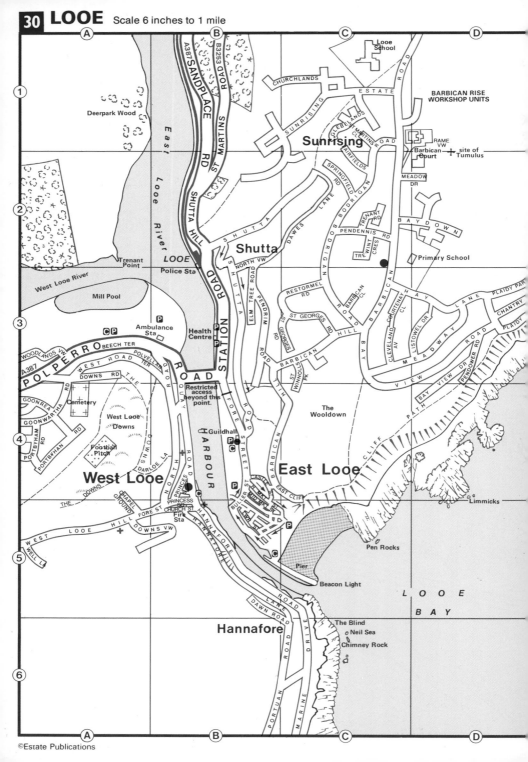

A   B   C   D

1

Deerpark Wood

East Looe River

Looe School

CHURCHLANDS

ESTATE

BARBICAN RISE
WORKSHOP UNITS

Sunrising

SUNRISING

MEETINGS ROAD

GLEBELANDS CL

FAIRFIELDS

RAME VW
Barbican
Court

site of
Tumulus

MEADOW
DR

2

Trenant
Point

West Looe River

LOOE

Police Sta

Shutta

SHUTTA

NORTH VW

SHUTTA

SPRINGFIELD

DAWES LANE

BODRIGAN

TRENANT RD

TREWINT CRES

PENDENNIS RD

BAYDOWN

Primary School

Mill Pool

3

Ambulance
Sta

Health
Centre

CP

BEECH TER

POLVELLAN TER

WOODLANDS VW

POLPERRO

A387

DOWNS RD

THE

ELM TREE ROAD

WINDMILL

ST GEORGES RD

RESTORMEL
RD

ST GEORGES

BARBICAN
RD

BARBICAN CL

CLEVELAND AV

COURTENAY WAY

LISTOWEL DR

MEADWAY

BAY VIEW

PLAIDY PARK

CHANTRY

PLAIDY

ROAD

HILL

4

GOONREATH RD

GOONWARTHA RD

PORTBYHAN RD

PORTBYHAN

Cemetery

West Looe
Downs

Football
Pitch

DARLOE LA

DOWNS

CHAPEL GROUND

NORTH ROAD

PRINCES

DOWNS VW

West Looe

THE

DOWNS

WEST LOOE HILL

WELL L

STATION ROAD

QUAY

Restricted
access
beyond this
point.

Guildhall

FORE STREET

BULLER ST

CASTLE ST

East Looe

The
Wooldown

BARBICAN PK

ST WINNOLLS

HILL

CLIFF PATH

PENOWER RD

Limmicks

5

PRINCESS
RD
CHURCH ST
Fire
Sta

Fore St

HANNAFORE

HARBOUR

ROAD

Pier

Pen Rocks

Beacon Light

LOOE
BAY

6

Hannafore

CHAPEL
GROUND

DAWN ROAD

PORTUAN ROAD

MARINE DRIVE

HANNAFORE ROAD

LANE

The Blind
Neil Sea
Chimney Rock

A   B   C   D

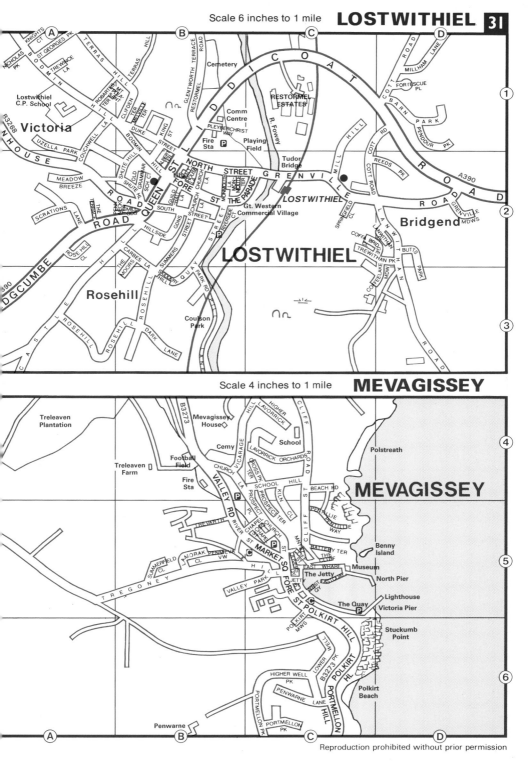

LOSTWITHIEL

Victoria

Lostwithiel C.P. School

Rosehill

Coulson Park

Bridgend

MEVAGISSEY

Treleaven Plantation

Treleaven Farm

Mevagissey House

Polstreath

Benny Island

Museum

North Pier

The Jetty

The Quay

Lighthouse

Victoria Pier

Stuckumb Point

Polkirt Beach

Penwarne

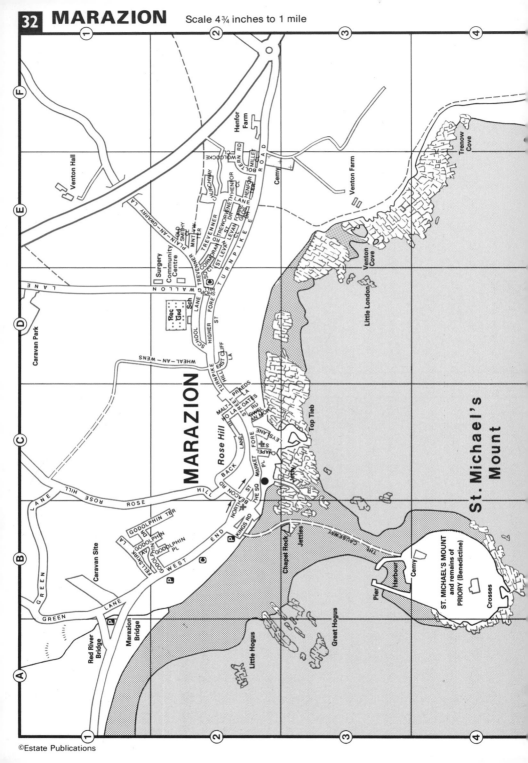

MARAZION

32

Scale 4¾ inches to 1 mile

St. Michael's Mount

MARAZION

Rose Hill

ST. MICHAEL'S MOUNT
and remains of
PRIORY (Benedictine)

Venton Hall

Caravan Park

Caravan Site

Red River Bridge

Marazion Bridge

Little Hogus

Great Hogus

Chapel Rock

Jetties

The Causeway

Pier

Harbour

Cemy

Crosses

Little London

Venton Cove

Venton Farm

Trenow Cove

Henfor Farm

Cemy

Surgery

Community Centre

Rec Grd

Sch

Top Tieb

GREEN LANE

ROSE HILL LANE

ROSE HILL

GODOLPHIN TER

GODOLPHIN AV

GODOLPHIN PL

FELLSHIR LA

WEST END

GREEN LANE

KINGS RD

BEACON RD

NORTH RD

THE SQ

MARKET PL

FORE ST

CHAPEL PL

LEYS LANE

GWEL AN MOR

ST. THOMAS LA

PRAEDS

TURNPIKE

HILL

WHEAL-AN-WENS

EAST CLIFF LA

SCHOOL LANE

HIGHER FORE ST

SHOP LANE

TURNPIKE

WALLON LANE

PLAIN-AN-GWARRY LA

TREVENNER LA

GOLD SMITHY ROW

MNT-VW

SOCIETY

ST LEVAN

TREVENEV

DR

HENFOR

GEORGE

FORE

LEVAN

HENFOR CL

CHURCHWAY

KERN RD

WOOLOCKE

MILL

BOL

ROAD

MALT HO LA

BACK LANE

ROSE HILL

Venton Hall

©Estate Publications

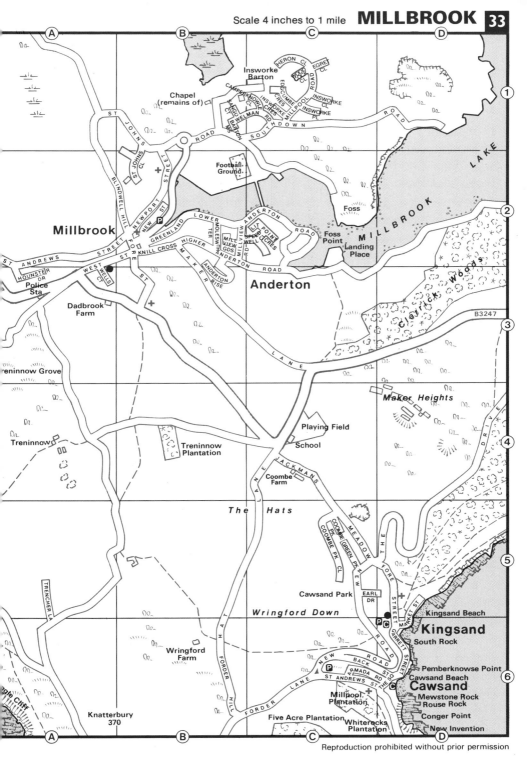

A B C D

1

INSWORKE BARTON
Chapel (remains of)
HERON CL
EGRET CL
EDGCUMBE RD
WOOD CL
MILLPOOL ROAD
INSWORKE CL
INSWORKE PT
CAMPERDOWN CRES
INSWORKE CRES
ST JOHNS ST
BARTON BELMAN MS
SOUTH DOWN ROAD

2

Millbrook
ST JOHNS CL
NEWPORT STREET
GREENLAND
LOWER MOLESWORTH TER
MILLVIEW GDNS
ANDERTON ROAD
LIT POINT
SPEY CRES
WELL
Foss
Foss Point
Landing Place
MILLBROOK LAKE

ST ANDREWS STREET
HOUNSTER DR
Police Sta
WEST WELLS
KNILL CROSS
HIGHER ANDERTON ROAD
MAKER RISE
Anderton
Dadbrook Farm
MAKER LANE
B3247

3

Treninnow Grove
Treninnow
Treninnow Plantation
Maker Heights

4

Playing Field
School
JACKMANS LANE
Coombe Farm
DRIVE

The Hats

5

Wringford Farm
MEADOW
COOMBE GREEN PK CL
COOMBE PK CL
THE FORE STREET
NEW ROAD
EARL DR
Cawsand Park
Kingsand Beach
Kingsand
South Rock
GARRETT STREET
MARKET ST

6

TRENCHER LA
Wringford Down
HAT LANE
FORDER HILL
FORDER LANE
NEW ST
BACK ST
ARMADA RD
ST ANDREWS ST
Millpool Plantation
Five Acre Plantation
Whiteracks Plantation
Pemberknowse Point
Cawsand Beach
Cawsand
Mewstone Rock
Rouse Rock
Conger Point
New Invention

Knatterbury 370

Eagle Cliff

A B C D

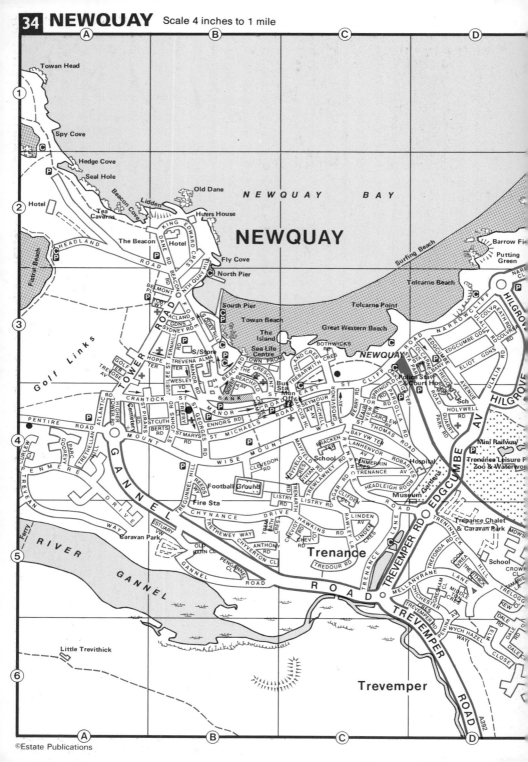

Towan Head

Spy Cove

Hedge Cove

Seal Hole

Old Dane

Beacon Cove

Liddon

NEWQUAY   BAY

Tea Caverns

Huers House

Hotel

NEWQUAY

The Beacon

Hotel

Fly Cove

Barrow Fie

Putting Green

Surfing Beach

North Pier

South Pier

Towan Beach

The Island

Sea Life Centre

Tolcarne Beach

Tolcarne Point

Great Western Beach

BOTHWICK'S

NEWQUAY

Police Sta
& Court Ho

Sch

HILGRO

HILGROVE

Golf Links

S/Store

Bus Sta

Post Office

Mini Railway

Trenance Leisure P
Zoo & Waterwor

Hospital

Cemetery

Football Ground

Fire Sta

School

Museum

Gardens

Trenance Chalet
& Caravan Park

School

Caravan Park

Trenance

Fistral Beach

Little Trevithick

RIVER   GANNEL

Trevemper

©Estate Publications

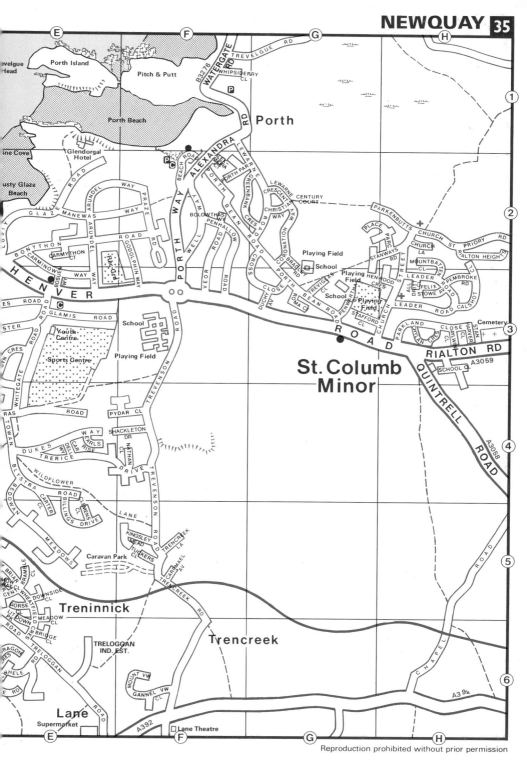

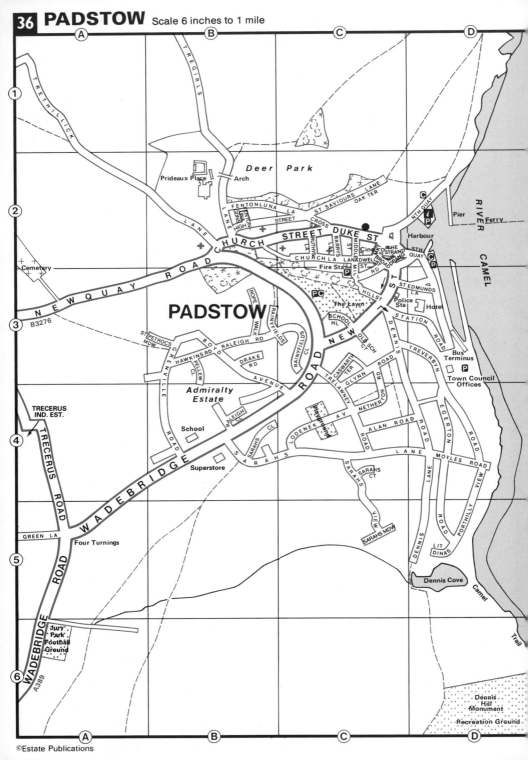

©Estate Publications

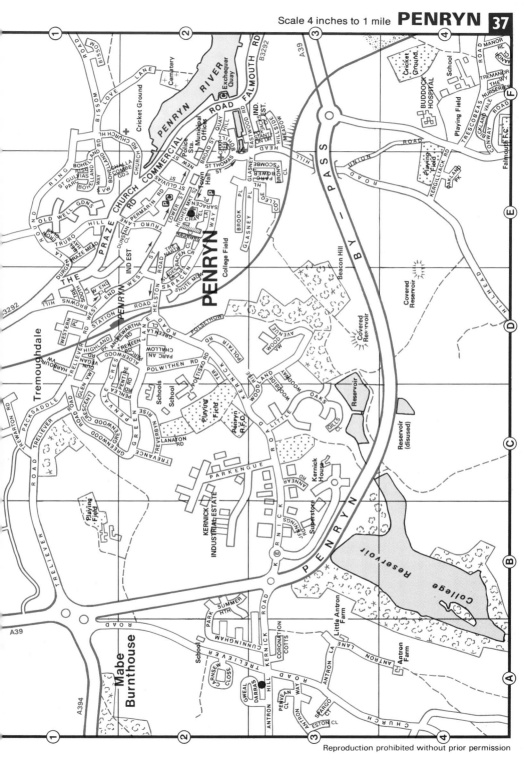

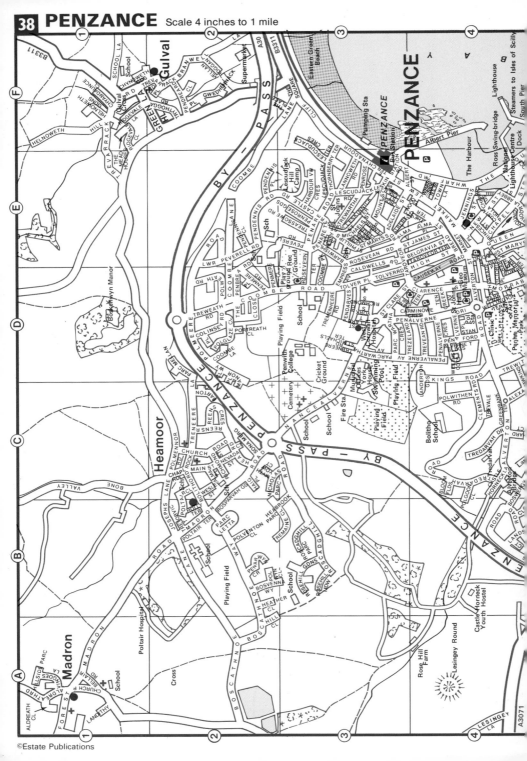

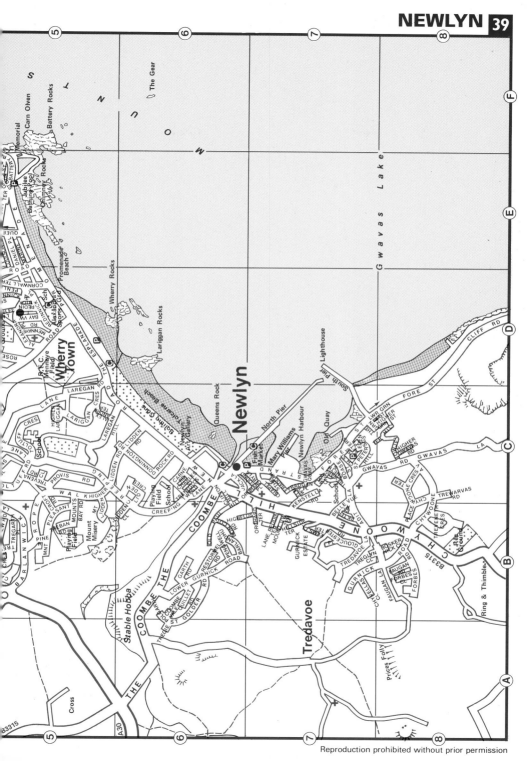

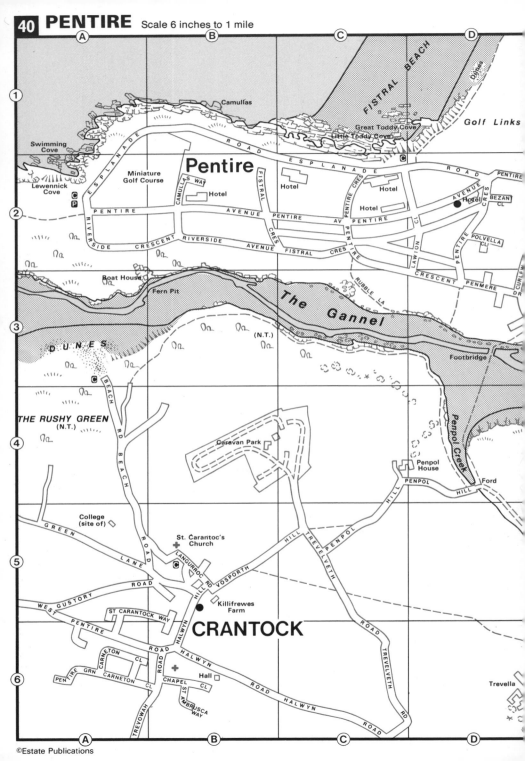

FISTRAL BEACH

Camullas

Great Toddy Cove
Little Toddy Cove

Golf Links

Ditties

Swimming
Cove

ESPLANADE ROAD

Pentire

ROAD ESPLANADE ROAD PENTIRE

Lewennick
Cove

Miniature
Golf Course

CAMULLAS WAY

Hotel

Hotel

Hotel

Hotel

Hotel

PENTIRE CRES

PENTIRE CRES

BEZANT CL

PENTIRE AVENUE

POLVELLA CLI

RIVERSIDE CRESCENT

PENTIRE AVENUE

PENTIRE CRES

PENTIRE AV

FISTRAL CRES

PENTIRE

LAWTON CL

AVENUE

CRESCENT PENMERE

CURLEW DR

ESPLANADE

PENTIRE

RIVERSIDE AVENUE

FISTRAL CRES

Boat House

Fern Pit

The Gannel

RUBBLE LA

(N.T.)

Footbridge

DUNES

Penpol Creek

THE RUSHY GREEN
(N.T.)

BEACH RD

Caravan Park

Penpol
House

Ford

PENPOL HILL HILL

College
(site of)

GREEN LANE

ROAD

St. Carantoc's
Church

LANGURROC RD

HILL YOSPORTH

PENPOL HILL

TREVELVETH

WEST GUSTORY ROAD

ST CARANTOCK WAY

Killifrewes
Farm

CRANTOCK

ROAD TREVELVETH RD

Trevella

WEST PENTIRE

HALWYN

CARNETON CL

PEN TIRE GRN

CARNETON CL

ROAD HALWYN

CHAPEL ST

ST AMBRUSCA WAY

Hall

ROAD HALWYN ROAD

TREVOWAH RD

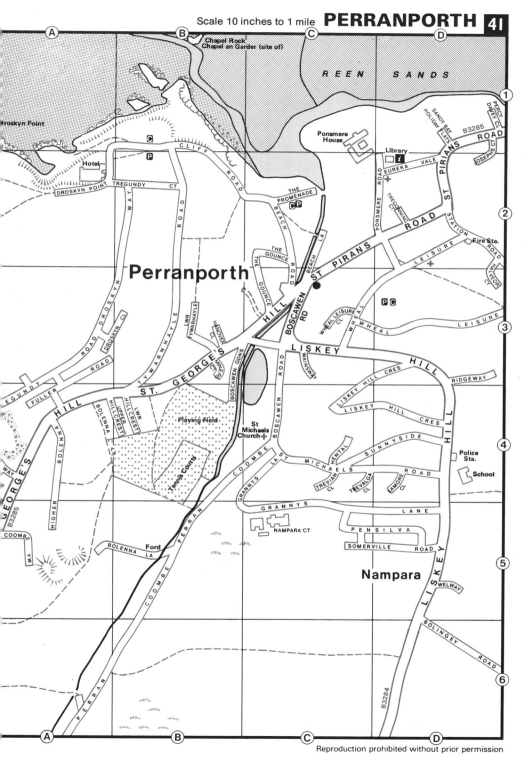

Paynter's Lane End

SPARNON GATE

Gilbert's Coomb

HARRIS MILL

BASSETT ROAD

PENWARTHA RD
PENRY VEAN
PENCROWN
POLDARK
TOLGUS
VALLEY GDNS
LAMANVA RDS
RICHARDS
BASSETT
MERRITTS HILL
BEACON VW PK

Vogue Beloth

TRELVELTHAN RD
BOSVEAN GDNS
RICHARDS LANE
KESTREL WAY
PARR
LANE
Football Ground

Lwr West Tolgus

Sunnyside
PARC
SUNNYSIDE
SPREYSEN
CLIFTON RD
SPAR LANE
LEVEN
PARK
LOWER BROAD LANE
FERRITTS
WEST TOLGUS

HIGHER WEST TOLGUS

TOLSKITHY VALLEY

Disused Mine

TOLGUS

SCORRIER

NEW PORTREATH ROAD
PORTREATH ROAD
B3300

Broad Lane

SYCAMORE DR
FORTH AN PRAZE
GRENIFER RD

CAMBORNE

Old Shafts

REDRUTH BY PASS

TOLGUS VEAN
Super
School
MOUNT

A30

NORTH POOL RD
HIGHER BROAD LANE
TRELOWEY WAY
KILLERS RD
CHAPEL
BALKIN
HARRISON GDNS
WAY
CHYNOON GDNS
MENKAYE GDNS
School

TOLSKITHY VALLEY

Disused Mines

TAREWASTE

School

Moorfield
WHEAL AGAR
TRELONETH
TANGYE RD
TREVITHICK RD
EAST POOL PK
KILLIERS RD
BOSWEOR PARK
BROAD LANE
FORTUNE LA
STAMPS LA
CHARIOT CL
CHILL
WHEAL KINDALE CL
ROE
AG4
CRES

Illogan Highway

Supermkt
AGAR
ROAD

Chapel
ELM CL
ROE
CL
School
CRIBLING WELL
WHEAL TEHIDY LA
WHEAL BARNCOOSE TER
BARNCOOSE TER

BARNCOOSE TER

REDRUTH
WEST PK
BLOWINGHOUSE
RIVER ROW
SOUTH PK
RAILWAY VILLAS
SOUTH PK CL
TRE
WINGET
CRES
CHURCH LA
TREVING

Chapel
DRUIDS ROAD
Playing Field
BARNCOOSE LA
CAMBORNE & REDRUTH COMMUNITY HOSPITAL
BARNCOOSE IND. EST.

POOL INDUSTRIAL ESTATE
AGAR WAY
WILSON
HIGHBURROW LA
TITHE WAY

Disused Mines

Old Shafts
Old Shafts
Old Shafts

Giants Well

CARN BREA VILLAS
CARN BREA
VILLAS
TUNY CRES
Chapel
WEST TREVINGEY TER
TREVANION TER
St. Uny Church

Chu

Carn Brea Village

Carnbrea Castle
Hill Fort

CARN BREA

Tregajorran

COOMBE
REDRUTH

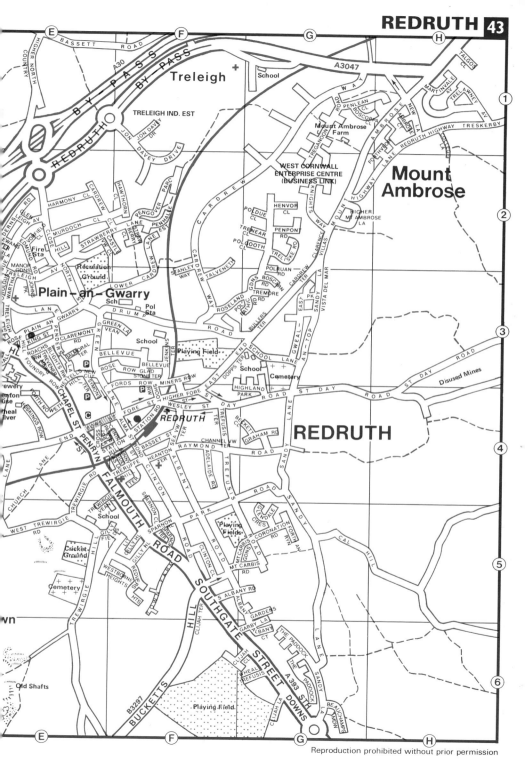

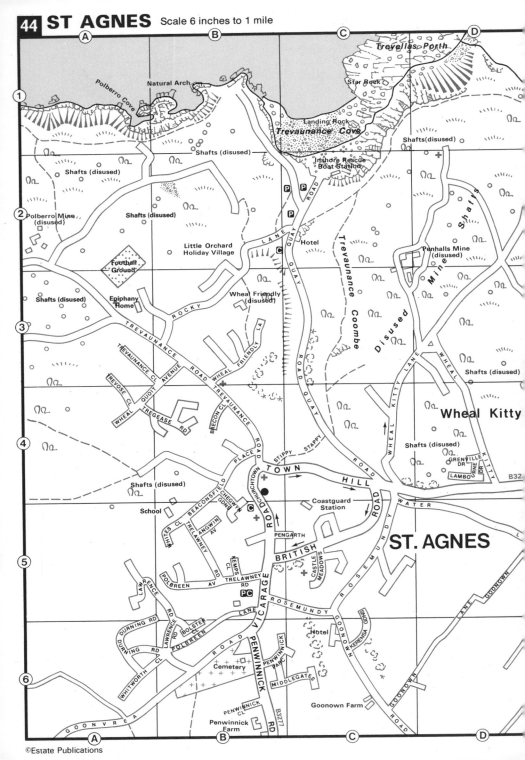

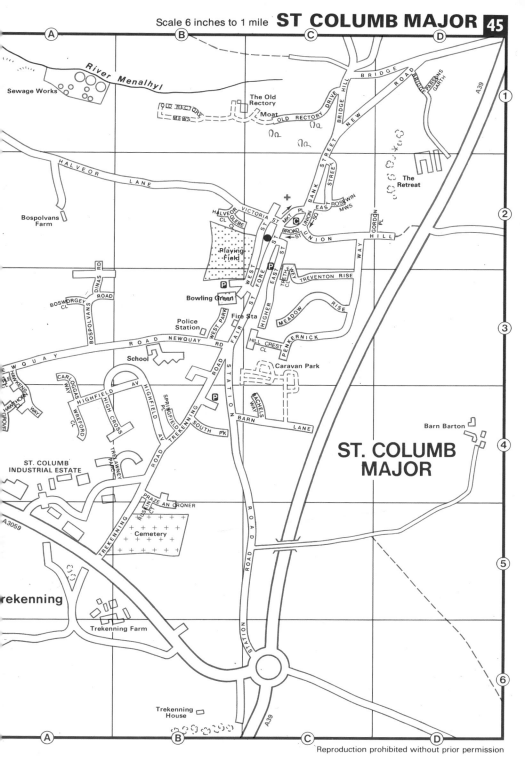

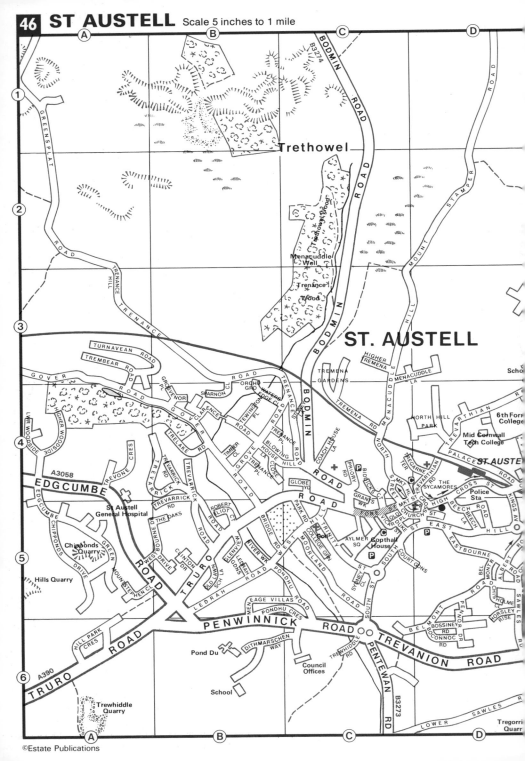

Trethowel

ST. AUSTELL

Menacuddle Well

Trenance Wood

Trethowel Wood

BODMIN ROAD

B3274

GREENSPLAT ROAD

TRENANCE HILL

TRENANCE ROAD

TURNAVEAN ROAD

TREMBEAR ROAD

GOVER ROAD

HIGHER WOODSIDE

LWR WOODSIDE

EDGCUMBE

A3058

REVONE CRES

EDGCUMBE ROAD

CHIPPONDS DRIVE

GREEN

Chipponds Quarry

Hills Quarry

TRELAKE RD

TREVARRICK RD

TREVARRICK

TREVARRICK ROAD

THE OAKS

WEST BOURNE DRIVE

MOUNTSTEPHEN CL

TRURO ROAD

LEDRAH ROAD

CLINTON DR

OLD LAWN

GLENVIEW GDNS

ST AUSTELL GARDENS

SPARNON CL

GROVE

GLOVER ROAD

LAURENCE CL

TREWIGTON PL

TIMBER CL

GROVE ROAD

ORCHID GRO

WATERS EDGE CL

TRENANCE ROAD

BLOWING HOUSE HILL

TRENANCE PL

GLOBE YD

GRANTS WK

PARK RD

BRIDGE RD

RIVER WK

PONDHU ROAD

MOORLAND ROAD

COLLEGE GRN

BIDDICKS CL

PRIORY RD

COACH HOUSE LA

ST AUSTELL General Hospital

ROBERT CLIOT

TREMENA GARDENS

HIGHER TREMENA

TREMENA RD

NORTH STREET

BODMIN ROAD

MENACUDDLE LA

MENACUDDLE

NORTH HILL PARK

TREVARTHIAN RD

BEGARNE TER

CROSS ST

PALACE RD

6th Form College

Mid Cornwall Tech College

ST AUSTE

Scho

THE SYCAMORES

HIGH ST

Police Sta

MKT HL

TREVARTHIAN

CHURCH ST

EAST HILL

BEECH RD

BEECH LA

KINGS AV

EASTBOURNE

BELMONT TER

ALBERT

BEL MONT RD

BOSSINEY RD

CONNOC RD

PENROR DR

HORSLEY RISE

HOLME

SAWLES RD

SOUTH ST

COURT GDNS

AYLMER SQ

SYDNEY ST

Copthall House

Trinity School

PENWINNICK ROAD

TREVANION ROAD

HILL PARK CRES

A390

TRURO ROAD

Pond Du

DITHMARSCHEN WAY

MENEAGE VILLAS

PONDHU CRES

Council Offices

School

TREWHIDDLE RD

PENTEWAN RD

B3273

LOWER SAWLES RD

Trewhiddle Quarry

Tregorri Quarr

ST AUSTELL 47

Boscoppa

Bethel

Mount Charles

NORTH EAST DISTRIBUTION RD

HOLMBUSH ROAD

SOUTHBOURNE ROAD

CROMWELL RD

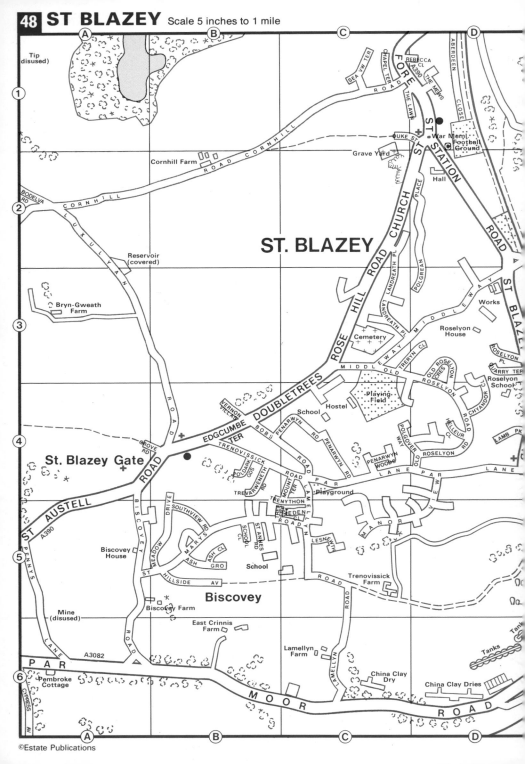

ST. BLAZEY

St. Blazey Gate

Biscovey

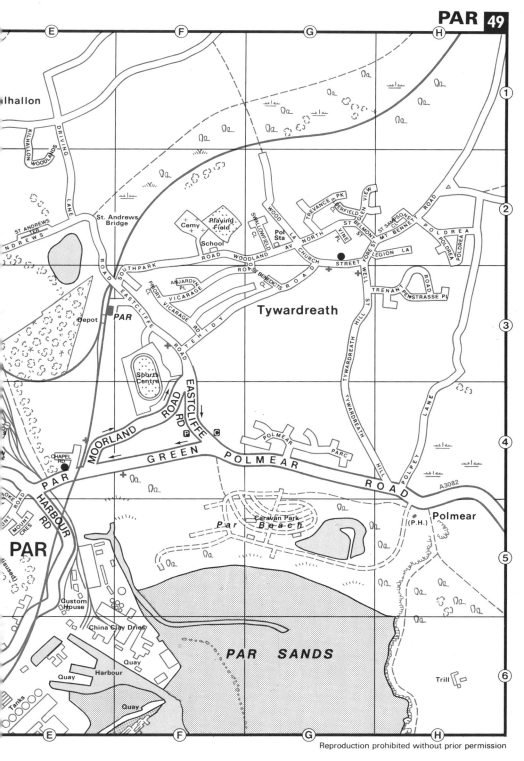

E F G H

1
2
3
4
5
6

lhallon

KILHALLON WOODLANDS
DRIVING LANE

ST ANDREWS TER
ANDREWS

St. Andrews Bridge

ROAD
SOUTHPARK
EASTCLIFFE

Depot

PAR

PRIORY
VICARAGE
TEHIDY ROAD

ROAD

Sports Centre

MOORLAND ROAD
EASTCLIFFE RD

P C

Cemy
Playing Field
School

SWALLOWFIELD CL

WOOD LA NORTH

Pol Sta

AV
WOODLAND ROAD
BENEDICTS CL
ROAD
CHURCH ROAD

ANJARDYN PL

TREVANCE PK
BERFIELD
IGLEN VIEW
ST BELMONT ST SAMPSON
ST MT BENNETT ROAD

POLDREA
POLDREA
POLDREA

VINE
ST
PL

ST
FORE
STREET
WELL ST

LEGION LA

TRENANT
PENSTRASSE PL

ROAD

Tywardreath

TYWARDREATH HILL

TYWARDREATH HILL

POLPEY LANE

GREEN

POLMEAR

PAR

POLMEAR
PARC

ROAD

A3082

CHAPEL RD

PAR
HARBOUR RD

MOUNT CRES

PAR

Custom House

China Clay Dries

Quay
Harbour
Quay

Quay

Caravan Park

Par Beach

(P.H.)
Polmear

PAR SANDS

Trill

Tanks

E F G H

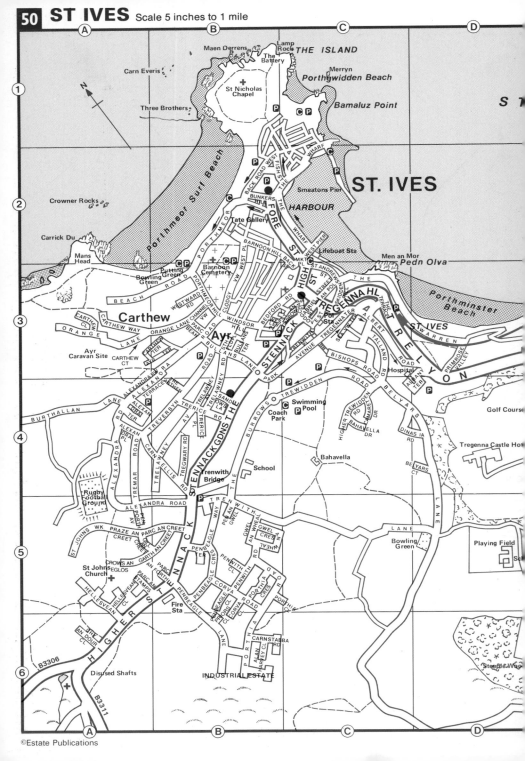

THE ISLAND

Maen Derrens
Lamp Rock
The Battery
Carn Everis
Merryn
Porthgwidden Beach
St Nicholas Chapel
Bamaluz Point
Three Brothers

ST. IVES

Smeatons Pier

Crowner Rocks

HARBOUR

Carrick Du

Tate Gallery

Men an Mor
Pedn Olva

Mans Head

Lifeboat Sta

Putting Green

Bowling Green

Barnoon Cemetery

Porthminster Beach

ST. IVES

Carthew

Ayr Caravan Site

Ayr

CARTHEW CT

TREGENNA HL

Hospital

Golf Course

Swimming Pool

Coach Park

Trewidden

Bahavella

Tregenna Castle Hotel

BURTHALLAN

School

Bahavella

Rugby Football Ground

Trenwith Bridge

Bowling Green

Playing Field

St Johns Church

Crows an Eglos

Fire Sta

Carnstabba

Disused Shafts

Steeple Way

B3306

B3311

INDUSTRIAL ESTATE

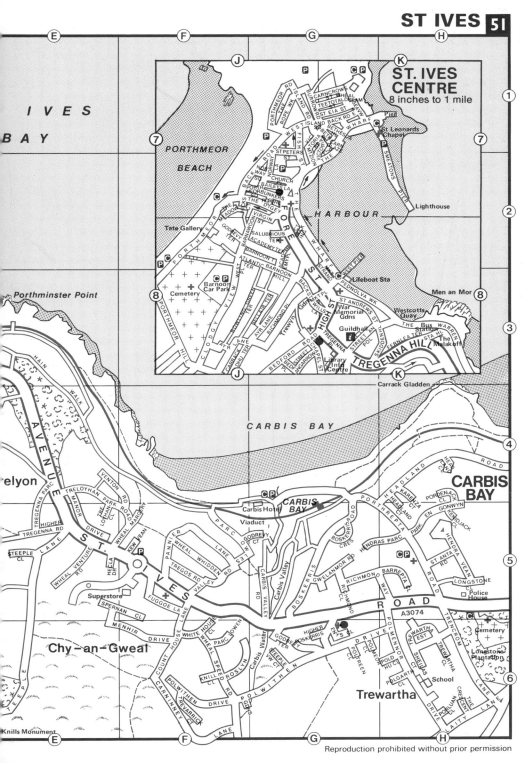

ST IVES 51

ST. IVES CENTRE
8 inches to 1 mile

IVES BAY

PORTHMEOR BEACH

Porthminster Point

HARBOUR

Lighthouse

Tate Gallery

St Leonards Chapel

Men an Mor

Cemetery

Barnoon Car Park

Lifeboat Sta

Westcotts Quay

War Memorial Gdns

Bus Station

The Malakoff

Guildhall

TREGENNA HILL

Library/Info Centre

Carrack Gladden

CARBIS BAY

AVENUE

elyon

Carbis Hotel

CARBIS BAY Viaduct

CARBIS BAY

ST. IVES

Superstore

Chy-an-Gweal

Trewartha

Police House

Cemetery

Longstone Plantation

School

Knills Monument

Disused Mine

B3306

NO GO BY HILL

NANCHERROW ROW

Tregeseal

NANCHERROW

Disused Mine

OLD FOUNDRY

TREGESEAL TER

TREGESEAL ROW

TREGESEAL

Ford

Disused Mine

NANCHERROW ROW

NANCHERROW HILL

NANCHERROW TER

Rugby Football Ground

THE TURNPIKE

NEW

Cross (remains of)

BOSWEDDEN

PEDNANDREA

Cemetery

CHAPEL ROAD

Methodist Chapel

Town Hall

NORTH ROW

ROAD

CHAPEL STREET

VENTON EAST HILL

ROAD

School

CHAPEL RD

BOSWEDDEN RD

BANK SQ

Kings Arms

St. Just's Church

CAPE

CORNWALL ROAD

Sch

Cape CORNWALL ST

CHURCH ST

VENTON E SO

TER

CORNWALL

ROAD

Amphitheatre Plain-an-Gwary

MKT SQ P

ST. JUST

PLEASANT

PRINCESS ST

QUEEN ST

VICTORIA ROW

WEST PLACE

STREET

Fire Sta

Library

FORE

BETHAN PL

CAPE

BOSORNE

TER

MARKET

c

STREET

P

LAFROWDA CL

Methodist Chapel

BOSORNE ST

BOSORNE TERRACE

LAFROWDA TER

PENZANCE

REGENT TER

BOSORNE RD

VOUNDER GLAZE

SOUTH

PLACE

ROAD

A3071

SOUTH PL TER

SOUTH GDS

CARN BOSAVERN CL

CARRALLACK

CARRALLACK MEWS

CARRALLACK TER

CARN BOSAVERN

Cemet

CARRALLACK LANE

CARRALLACK TER

Carrallack

Carn Bosavern

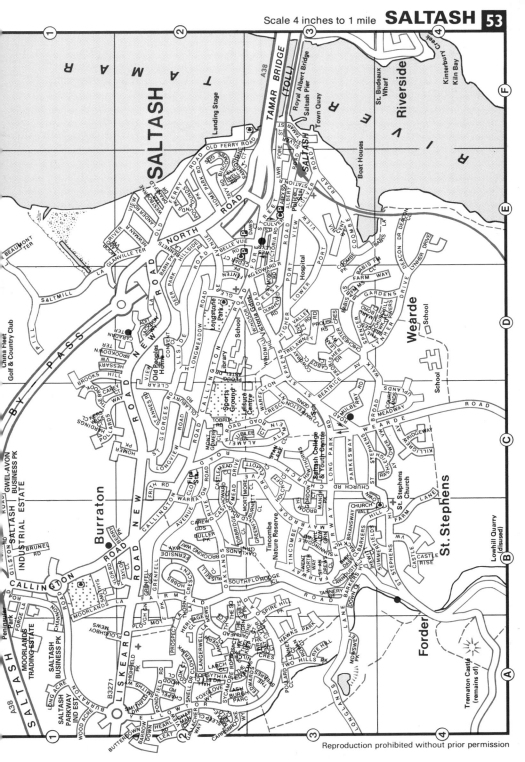

A B C D

1

Lodge

Westdown
Cottage

ANTONY

Gimpson Wood

Binney's
Plantation

Borough Farm
House

THE MEADOWS

2

Horson
Cottages

Sports Ground

Borough
Court

TREVITHIC

PRIMROSE CL

KYHANCE CL

A374

BOROUGH PK

BOROUGH LA

AV

INCE CL

FISTRAL
GWITHIN

CARLTON

AVENUE

SENNEN

LAMORNA PARK

PENLEE PK

GROVE PK

ROAD

KERNOWD

LANGDON DOWN

TREMATON

CARLYON

CARLYON

3

HORSON
CEMETERY

TALBOT WAY

FISGARD WAY

FROBISHER
WAY

WAY

FISGARD WAY

Sports Ground

TRELAWNEY WAY

WAVISH PK

CL

CLEGG AV

ADAMS CRES

WESTLAKE CL

PENDENNIS

PENTIRE

TREVITHIC

DAVY CL

GURNEY CL

TREVOL BUSINESS PARK

**H.M.S.
FISGARD**

TRELAWNEY RISE

ADAMS RISE

MURDOCK RD

GOAD CL

TRENGROUSE AV

AVENUE

4

TREVOL

Trevol
House

ROAD

TREVOL PL

TREVOL

HAWTHORN CL

PENCAIR AV

TREGONING RD

TREVORDER RD

CEDAR CL

CEDAR DR

CEDAR DR

PENDILLY AV

ROAD

5

H.M.S. RALEIGH
(Naval Training Establishment)

Trevol Sports Ground

TREVOL RIFLE RANGE

6

Sewage Works

Eastdowns Lake

Targets

Deadmans
Point

A B C D

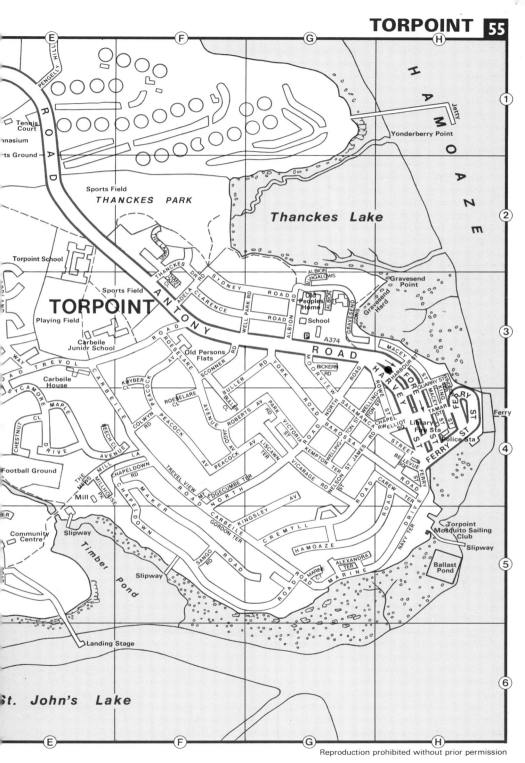

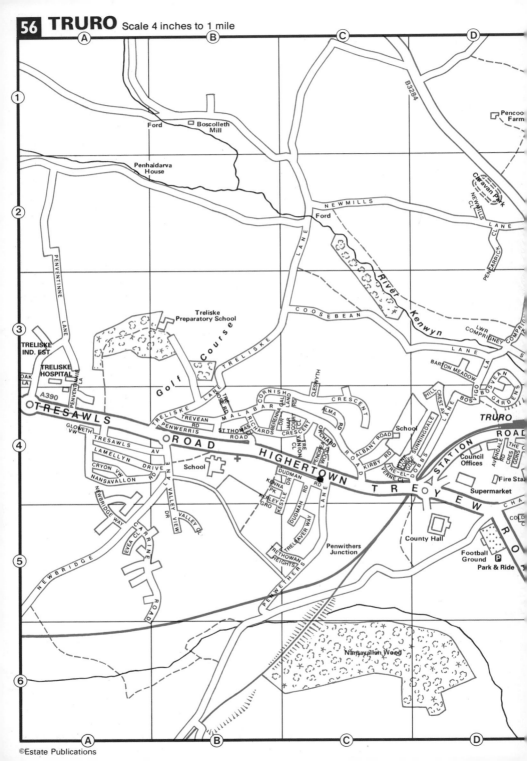

A B C D

1
2
3
4
5
6

Ford
Boscolleth Mill

Penhaldarva House

B3284

Pencoo Farm

Caravan Park
NEWMILLS CL

NEWMILLS LANE

Ford

River Kenwyn

PENARRICK

COOSEBEAN

LWR COMPRIBNEY
LANE
COMPRIB

Treliske Preparatory School

BARTON MEADOW LA

Golf Course

TRELISKE LANE

TRELISKE IND. EST.

OAK LA

TRELISKE HOSPITAL

PENVENTINNE LA

A390

PENVENTINNE LANE

TRESAWLS ROAD

GLOWETH VW

TRELISKE RD

TREVEAN RD

PENWERRIS ROAD

ST THOMAS RD

MALABAR RD

CORNISH RD

ORCHARDS

BERENNA DR

CLIFF RD

CLEGWYTH

ALMA

CRESCENT

School

TRURO

STATION ROAD

BOSVEAN GARDENS

HILL
CRESANT
LANE
BOS

AVONDALE
CRES
GDNS

THE C
CDNS

TRESAWLS AV

LAMELLYN RD

CRYON VW

NANSAVALLON

DRIVE

VALLEY DR

VALLEY CL

School

ORCHARD

CRESCENT

PENGELLY RD

ALBANY ROAD

KIRBY RD

VERNE RD

THE-EL-C

COBBS

SUNNINGDALE

CLOSE

TREYEW

Council Offices

Fire Stal

Supermarket

NEWBRIDGE WAY

NANSAVALLON RD

EVEA CL

CARRINE RD

NEWBRIDGE ROAD

KENNA PK

KESTLE

HENLEY GRO

DUDMAN DR

DUDMAN RD

KENNA LANE

PENHELLAF

TREBARVER WAY

TRETHOWANS HEIGHTS

Penwithers Junction

PENWETHER

County Hall

Football Ground
Park & Ride
P

COLD

CHA

ROA

Nansavallan Wood

A B C D

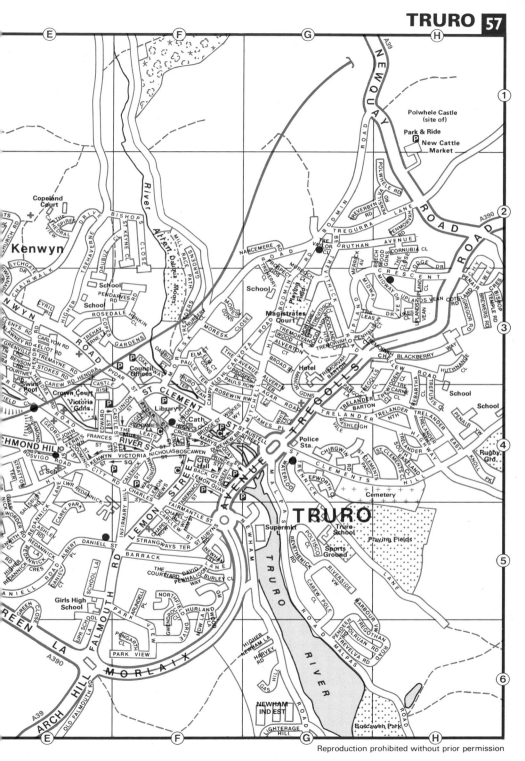

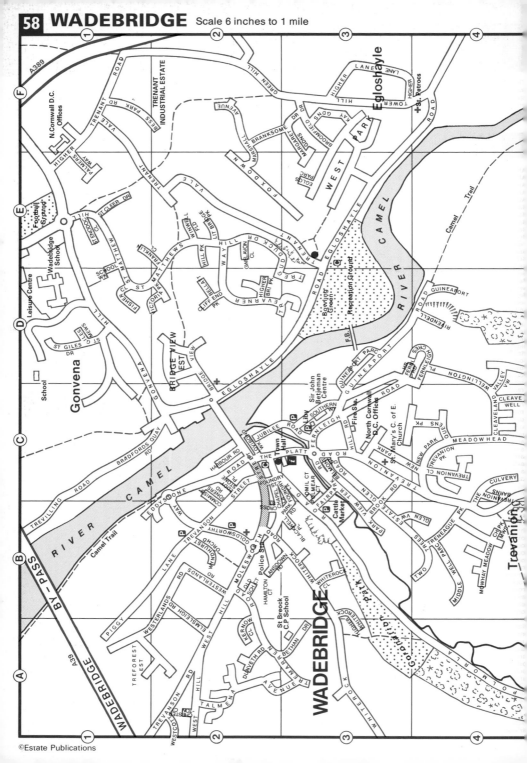

A - Z INDEX TO STREETS

with Postcodes

he Index includes some names or which there is insufficient pace on the maps. These names re preceded by an * and are ollowed by the nearest adjoining horoughfare.

BODMIN

bbots Clo. PL31 13 G4
lexandra Rd. PL31 12 B2
n Gof Gdns. PL31 12 D3
rmchair Corner. PL31 12 D1
thelstan Park. PL31 13 G4
arn La. PL31 12 C3
arrie Cres. PL31 13 E5
awden Rd. PL31 12 B5
eacon Clo. PL31 12 D3
eacon Hill. PL31 13 E3
eacon Lanes. PL31 12 D3
eacon Rd. PL31 12 D3
eatrice Rd. PL31 13 H6
ederkesa Ct. PL31 12 D3
eech Dri. PL31 12 B3
ell La. PL31 13 E2
eraton Ct. PL31 13 E2
erry La. PL31 13 F1
erry Towers. PL31 13 G1
errycombe Hill. PL31 12 C1
errycombe Rd. PL31 12 D1
errycombe Vale. PL31 12 B1
erryfields Est. PL31 13 E1
erryfields House. PL31 13 E2
lowinghouse La. PL30 12 A6
odiniel Rd. PL31 12 C1
odiniel View. PL31 12 B2
osvenna View. PL31 13 E4
oundary Road. PL31 12 A3
oxwell Park. PL31 13 G3
ramley Park. PL31 13 G2
ree Shute La. PL31 13 E2
roomfield Dri. PL31 12 B4
rowning Dri. PL31 12 B5
urden Clo. PL31 12 C4
urnards Ct. PL31 13 E2
urnards La. PL31 12 D2
ardell Rd. PL31 12 D1
arpenter Ct. PL31 13 E1
astle Canyke Rd. PL31 13 F4
astle Hill Ct. PL31 13 F1
astle Hill Gdns. PL31 13 G1
astle St. PL31 13 F2
elia Heights. PL31 13 G5
hapel La. PL31 13 E2
herry Tree Clo. PL31 12 B3
hestnut Gro. PL31 12 B3
hurch La. PL31 13 F2
hurch Park. PL31 13 G2
hurch Sq. PL31 13 F2
oldharbour La. PL31 13 G5
ooksland La. PL31 13 H1
opthorn Rd. PL31 12 D1
orporation Rd. PL31 12 B3
rabtree La. PL31 12 C6
rinnicks Hill. PL31 13 E3
rockwell St. PL31 13 F2
ross La. PL31 13 F1
awe Cres. PL31 12 C5
ennison Rd. PL31 13 E2
onely Ct. PL31 12 D1
unmere Rd. PL31 12 A2
izabeth Clo. PL31 12 D3
nn V.C. Estate. PL31 12 D2
amank Park. PL31 12 C3
axmoor Terr. PL31 12 D1
ore St. PL31 13 E2
oster Rd. PL31 12 B5
oulston Way. PL31 12 B3
urze Hill. PL31 13 E1
ilbert Rd. PL31 13 H4
ladstone Rd. PL30 12 B6
reen La. PL31 13 E6
regorys Ct. PL31 12 D2
algavor Rd. PL31 13 E6
algavor View. PL31 13 G6
arleigh Rd. PL31 13 F4
armer Clo. PL31 13 E1
Higher Bore St. PL31 12 C2
Hillside Park. PL31 12 D2
Homefield Pk. PL31 13 H4
Honey St. PL31 13 F2

INDUSTRIAL & RETAIL:

Bodmin Business Centre. PL31 13 F5
Walker Lines Ind Est. PL31 13 G6

Jago Clo. PL31 12 B5
Kay Cres. PL31 12 B4
Kerhuon Ct. PL31 12 D2
Kernow Clo. PL31 13 H2
Kinsman Estate. PL31 12 C5
Kirland Rd. PL30 12 B5
Lanhydrock Vw. PL31 13 E5
Launceston Clo. PL31 13 H3
Launceston Rd. PL31 13 G3
Leafield. PL31 13 H2
Little Meadow. PL31 13 E1
Lostwithiel Rd. PL31 13 F4
Love La. PL31 13 G2
Lower Bore St. PL31 12 D2
Lucas Clo. PL31 13 E4
Lucknow Rd. PL31 13 H6
Lynwood Clo. PL31 13 E4
Maple Clo. PL31 12 B3
Margaret Cnr. PL31 12 D2
Margaret Cres. PL31 12 D3
Market St. PL31 13 E2
Marks Dri. PL31 13 F4
Marshall Rd. PL31 13 E5
Martins Ct. PL31 13 E2
Mayfield. PL31 13 H2
Meadow Pl. PL31 13 E3
Midway Rd. PL31 12 A2
Mill St. PL31 13 E2
Monument Way. PL31 12 C3
Moor Vw. PL31 13 G6
Mount Folly. PL31 13 F2
Normandy Way. PL31 13 G6
Northey Rd. PL31 13 E3
Oakwood Pk. PL31 13 H2
Old Callywith Rd. PL31 13 G1
Old Market Pl. PL31 12 B3
Omaha Rd. PL31 13 G5
Opies La. PL31 12 C2
Paardeburg Rd. PL31 13 H6
Park Dri. PL31 12 B3
Paull Rd. PL31 12 B3
Penbugle La. PL31 13 F1
Penquite Dri. PL31 13 H2
Pethybridge Dri. PL31 12 B5
Pool St. PL31 13 E2
Pound La. PL31 13 F2
Priory Rd. PL31 13 F2
Queens Cres. PL31 12 B4
Radnor Clo. PL31 13 G4
Ranelagh Mews. PL31 13 E2
Respryn Rd. PL31 13 G6
Rhind St. PL31 13 F2
Robartes Rd. PL31 12 D3
Rock La. PL31 12 C4
Roman Dri. PL31 13 H6
Rosedale Gdns. PL31 13 H2
Roseland Gdns. PL31 13 F1
Roseland Rd. PL31 13 F1
Rosevallon La. PL31 12 C2
Rossett Gdns. PL31 13 H3
Rowan Clo. PL31 12 B3
St Dominic Clo. PL31 13 F1
St Georges Cres. PL31 12 C4
St Lawrence Rd. PL31 12 A3
St Leonards. PL31 12 C2
St Marys Clo. PL31 12 C3
St Marys Cres. PL31 12 C3
St Marys Rd. PL31 12 B5
St Mawgan Clo. PL31 13 H2
St Nicholas St. PL31 13 F3
St Petrocs Clo. PL31 13 F4
St Pirans Clo. PL31 12 B4
Sandra Way. PL31 12 B2
Scarletts Well Pk. PL31 12 C1
Scarletts Well Rd. PL31 12 A1
Sherwood Dri. PL31 12 B2
Springwell Vw. PL31 13 G2
Statham Rd. PL31 12 D3
Sycamore Clo. PL31 12 B3
Tanwood View. PL31 12 C1
The Lodge. PL31 12 B3
Torwood Clo. PL31 12 D3
Tower Hill. PL31 13 F2
Tranquil La. PL31 12 C2
Tredanek Clo. PL31 12 B1
Tregullan Vw. PL31 13 E5
Trelawney Clo. PL31 12 C4
Trelawney Rd. PL31 12 B4
Tremayne Ho. PL31 12 B3
Treningle Vw. PL31 12 C5
Turf St. PL31 13 F2
Valley Vw. PL31 13 E5
Vivian Rd. PL31 12 B3
Wallace Mews. PL31 13 E1
Wallace Rd. PL31 12 D1
Westheath Av. PL31 12 A4
Westheath Rd. PL31 12 A4
Whitestone Cres. PL31 12 C4
Whitestone Rd. PL31 12 B4
Windsor Gro. PL31 13 H2
Windsor Mews. PL31 13 F2
Wingfield. PL31 13 H2

BUDE

Acland Clo. EX23 14 C1
Agnes Clo. EX23 14 D6
Arundel Ter. EX23 14 B5
Bagbury La. EX23 14 D6
Bede Haven Clo. EX23 14 C6
Belle Vue. EX23 14 B3
Belle Vue Av. EX23 14 B3
Belle Vue La. EX23 14 B3
Bencoolen Rd. EX23 14 C4
Berries Av. EX23 14 C5
Binhamy Clo. EX23 14 D5
Blanchminster Rd. EX23 14 C4
Bramble Hill. EX23 14 C3
Breakwater Rd. EX23 14 A3
Briar Rd. EX23 14 C5
Broadclose Hill. EX23 14 C3
Brook Dri. EX23 14 C1
Bulleid Way. EX23 14 C5
Burn View. EX23 14 B3
Cameron Clo. EX23 14 A1
Carteret Rd. EX23 14 C3
Catherine Clo. EX23 14 D6
Cedar Gro. EX23 14 C1
Ceres Ct. EX23 14 C5
Cherrill Gdns. EX23 14 C1
Church Path. EX23 14 A4
Clinton Clo. EX23 14 D5
Creathorne Rd. EX23 14 C1
Crooklets. EX23 14 A1
Crooklets Rd. EX23 14 A1
Downs View. EX23 14 B1
Durston Rd. EX23 14 C1
East Fairholme Rd. EX23 14 D2
Elm Dri. EX23 14 D4
Fairfield Rd. EX23 14 C4
Flexbury Av. EX23 14 C1
Flexbury Park. EX23 14 C2
Flexbury Park Ct. EX23 14 C2
Flexbury Park Rd. EX23 14 C2
Fosters Way. EX23 14 D2
Golf House Rd. EX23 14 B3
Granville Ter. EX23 14 B3
Gurney Clo. EX23 14 C1
Hallet Way. EX23 14 D1
Hartland Ter. EX23 14 B3
Hawthorn Av. EX23 14 D5
Hawthorn Clo. EX23 14 D5
Hollabury Rd. EX23 14 D1
Holnicote Rd. EX23 14 C3
Howards Way. EX23 14 C4

INDUSTRIAL & RETAIL:

Kings Hill Ind Est. EX23 14 D6
Pethericks Mill Ind Est. EX23 14 C6

Kenwyn Clo. EX23 14 B1
Kernow Cres. EX23 14 D6
Killerton Rd. EX23 14 D4
King St. EX23 14 C3
Kings Hill. EX23 14 C5
Kings Hill Clo. EX23 14 C6
Lansdown Clo. EX23 14 C4
Lansdown Rd. EX23 14 C3
Lea Way. EX23 14 D2
Links Vw. EX23 14 D2
Lynstone Rd. EX23 14 B5
Maer Down. EX23 14 A1
Maer La. EX23 14 B1
Manor Rd. EX23 14 D5
Meadow Dri. EX23 14 D2
Minster Av. EX23 14 D5
Monterey Clo. EX23 14 C5
Ocean View Rd. EX23 14 B1
Pathfields. EX23 14 C4
Petherick Rd. EX23 14 B1
Pickard Way. EX23 14 B1
Poughill Rd. EX23 14 C1
Princes St. EX23 14 B3
Quarry Clo. EX23 14 C1
Queen St. EX23 14 C3
Redwood Clo. EX23 14 D4
Redwood Gro. EX23 14 D4
Seawell Rd. EX23 14 D1
Silverton Clo. EX23 14 C5
Silverton Rd. EX23 14 C4
Southfield Rd. EX23 14 C4
Stapleton Rd. EX23 14 D6
Stratton Ftpth. EX23 14 C4
Stratton Rd. EX23 14 C5
Summerleaze Av. EX23 14 B1
Summerleaze Cres. EX23 14 B3
The Crescent. EX23 14 B4
The Rowans. EX23 14 D5
The Strand. EX23 14 B4
Traly Clo. EX23 14 D6
Treleven Rd. EX23 14 D5
Trevella Rd. EX23 14 C1
Valley Rd. EX23 14 C5
Vicarage Rd. EX23 14 B5
Victoria Rd. EX23 14 B1
Warwick Rd. EX23 14 C5
West Fairholme Rd. EX23 14 C1
Westby Rd. EX23 14 C4
West Park Rd. EX23 14 B1
William Edwards Clo. EX23 14 D2
Woodfield Rd. EX23 14 D1

CALLINGTON

Amble Rd. PL17 15 D4
Aysshton Gdns. PL17 15 C4
Back La. PL17 15 B3
Beech Rd. PL17 15 C4
Biscombes La. PL17 15 B4
Broadmead. PL17 15 B3
Caradon Clo. PL17 15 B5
Cedar Clo. PL17 15 C4
Celtic Rd. PL17 15 D3
Chantry Pk. PL17 15 B4
Chapel St. PL17 15 B4
Chequetts Clo. PL17 15 B5
Church St. PL17 15 B3
Compton Rd. PL17 15 B3
Coombe Rd. PL17 15 D4
Coronation Rd. PL17 15 B3
Elm Clo. PL17 15 C4
Florence Hill. PL17 15 C1
Florence Rd. PL17 15 C1
Fore St. PL17 15 B4
Fowey Cres. PL17 15 D4
Frogwell Rd. PL17 15 A4
Glebe Rd. PL17 15 B2
Glebelands. PL17 15 B2
Glen Vw. PL17 15 B1
Granite Way. PL17 15 D3
Grenville Clo. PL17 15 B5
Guipavas Rd. PL17 15 D4
Hawthorne Clo. PL17 15 C4
Haye La. PL17 15 A1
Haye Rd. PL17 15 A3
Hazelwood Rd. PL17 15 C4

INDUSTRIAL & RETAIL:

Moss Side Ind Est. PL17 15 D3

Inney Clo. PL17 15 D4
Lamorna Dri. PL17 15 C3
Lansdowne Rd. PL17 15 A5
Launceston Rd. PL17 15 B1
Liskeard Rd. PL17 15 A4
Longfield Clo. PL17 15 D3
Lower Coronation Ter. PL17 15 B3
Lynher Way. PL17 15 D4
Maple Clo. PL17 15 C4
Market Sq. PL17 15 B4
Martin Sq. PL17 15 B4
Moonsfield. PL17 15 B4
New Rd. PL17 15 B4
Newport Clo. PL17 15 B3
Pengelly. PL17 15 C4
Penlee Clo. PL17 15 C3
Pollard Rd. PL17 15 B3
Porthmellon Gdns. PL17 15 C3
Rosemullion Gdns. PL17 15 C3
St Germans Rd. PL17 15 B5
St Therese Clo. PL17 15 C4
Saltash Rd. PL17 15 B4
Snells La. PL17 15 C1
South Hill Rd. PL17 15 A1
Southern Rd. PL17 15 A6
Tamar Clo. PL17 15 D3
Tavistock Rd. PL17 15 B4
Tors View Clo. PL17 15 C3
Trelawney Heights. PL17 15 C4
Trelawney Rise. PL17 15 C4
Trelawney Rd. PL17 15 B4
Trethurgy Gdns. PL17 15 B5
Urban Ter. PL17 15 B3
Valentine Row. PL17 15 A3
Well St. PL17 15 B3
Westover Rd. PL17 15 A5
Willow Clo. PL17 15 C4
Zaggy La. PL17 15 B3

CALSTOCK

Back Rd. PL18 18 B5
Baptist St. PL18 18 B5
Church Hill. PL18 18 B4
Church La. PL18 18 A5
Church St. PL18 18 B5
Commercial Rd. PL18 18 B5
Cothele Vw. PL18 18 A5
Eric Rd. PL18 18 D6
Fore St. PL18 18 B5
Harewood Rd. PL18 18 C6
Higher Kelly. PL18 18 A5
Johnson Park. PL18 18 A5
Lower Kelly. PL18 18 A5
Providence Pl. PL18 18 B5
Rose Hill Ter. PL18 18 A4
Rowse Gdns. PL18 18 B5
St Andrews Clo. PL18 18 B5
Sand La. PL18 18 A4
Station La. PL18 18 B5
Sunnyside. PL18 18 C5
Tamar Pl. PL18 18 B6
Tamar Ter. PL18 18 A5
*Tamar View, Tamar Pl. PL18 18 B6
The Adit. PL18 18 B6

CAMBORNE

Adelaide St. TR14 17 E4
Albert Pl. TR14 17 E3
Albert St. TR14 17 E3
Aneray Rd. TR14 17 E2
Atlantic Clo. TR14 17 F5
Atlantic Ter. TR14 17 F5
Barlowena. TR14 17 E5
Barripper Rd. TR14 16 C6
Bartles Row. TR14 17 H1
Basset Rd. TR14 16 D4
Basset St. TR14 16 D4
Beacon Fields. TR14 17 F5

Beacon Sq. TR14 — 17 G6
Beacon Ter. TR14 — 17 F5
Bekelege Dri. TR14 — 17 G6
Bellever Parc. TR14 — 17 F5
Bethany Homes. TR14 — 16 C5
Boundervean La. TR14 — 16 B5
Cadogan Clo. TR14 — 17 E6
Cadogan Dri. TR14 — 17 E6
Cadogan Rd. TR14 — 17 E6
Camborne Scorrier By Pass. TR14 — 16 A2
Carn_Av. TR14 — 17 F4
Carnarthen Rd. TR14 — 17 E4
Carnarthen St. TR14 — 17 E4
Carne View Clo. TR14 — 17 G1
Centenary Row Middle. TR14 — 17 E4
Centenary Row West. TR14
Centenary St. TR14 — 17 E4
Chapel Ct. TR14 — 17 F4
Chapel La. TR14 — 17 G4
Chapel St. TR14 — 16 D4
Chapel Ter. TR14 — 16 A2
Chenoweth Clo. TR14 — 16 B2
Choughs Clo. TR14 — 16 D4
Church La. TR14 — 16 D4
Church Rd, Penponds. TR14 — 16 A6
Church Rd, Treswithian. TR14 — 16 D4
Church St. TR14 — 16 D4
Church View Rd. TR14 — 17 G2
Chypraze St. TR14 — 16 A3
Cliff View Rd. TR14 — 17 E1
Cliff View Ter. TR14 — 17 E1
Clos Trevithick. TR14 — 17 F4
Codiford Cres. TR14 — 17 E2
College St. TR14 — 16 B3
Commercial Sq. TR14 — 16 D4
Commercial St. TR14 — 16 D4
Condurrow. TR14 — 17 H5
Condurrow Rd. TR14 — 17 G6
Coronation Av. TR14 — 16 B3
Cranberry Rd. TR14 — 16 B4
Crane Rd. TR14 — 16 B4
Cranfield Rd. TR14 — 16 B4
Cross St. TR14 — 17 E4
Dolcoath Av. TR14 — 17 F3
Dolcoath Dri. TR14 — 17 G3
Dolcoath Rd. TR14 — 17 H3
Dolcoath Rd. TR14 — 17 F3
East Charles St. TR14 — 17 E4
Eastern La. TR14 — 16 D2
Edward St. TR14 — 17 G1
Enys Rd. TR14 — 16 D2
Fairview Cotts. TR14 — 16 C4
Fernside Rd. TR14 — 16 A6
Fore St, Beacon. TR14 — 17 E5
Fore St, Camborne. TR14 — 16 D3
Fore St, Penponds. TR14 — 16 A6
Foundry Rd. TR14 — 17 F3
Garland Pl. TR14 — 16 D2
Gas St. TR14 — 16 D4
Gurneys La. TR14 — 16 D4
Gustavus St. TR14 — 16 D3
Gwelmor. TR14 — 17 F5
Hanover Ct. TR14 — 17 F2
Harefield Cres. TR14 — 16 D2
Hen Wythva. TR14 — 17 E5
Higher Pengegon. TR14 — 17 G4
Holman Av. TR14 — 16 B2
Hooper La. TR14 — 16 D4
Hughville St. TR14 — 17 E2
INDUSTRIAL ESTATE:
Formal Ind Pk. TR14 — 16 A2
Jethan Dri. TR14 — 16 B2
Jubilee Pl. TR14 — 17 F2
Jubilee Ter. TR14 — 17 E5
Kew Noweth. TR14 — 16 D5
Killivose Gdns. TR14 — 16 D6
Killivose Rd. TR14 — 16 D6
Kings Rd. TR14 — 16 D2
Langorran Rd. TR14 — 16 A2
Llawnroc Clo. TR14 — 17 F5
Lowenac Gdns. TR14 — 16 C4
Lower Pengegon. TR14 — 17 G3
Manor Rd. TR14 — 16 B4
Maynes Row. TR14 — 17 H1
Meadow Pl. TR14 — 16 B2
Meadow Vw. TR14 — 17 F6
Meneth Rd. TR14 — 17 F5
Mill Rd. TR14 — 16 A6

Mitchell La. TR14 — 17 E4
Mitchell Rd. TR14 — 16 B2
Moor St. TR14 — 17 E4
Morrab Rd. TR14 — 16 B4
Mount Pleasant Clo. TR14 — 17 E6
Mount Pleasant Rd. TR14 — 16 D5
Mount Pleasure. TR14 — 17 F6
New Connexion St. TR14 — 16 D4
Normandy Way. TR14 — 17 G4
North Parade. TR14 — 17 E3
North Parade Rear. TR14 — 17 E3
North Rd. TR14 — 17 E3
North Roskear Rd. TR14 — 17 E2
Parc Bracket St. TR14 — 17 E4
Parc an Bal Ct. TR14 — 17 F1
Parc an Tansys. TR14 — 17 G5
Parc Venton Clo. TR14 — 17 G4
Park an Bans. TR14 — 17 E6
Park an Gorsaf. TR14 — 16 D5
Park Holly. TR14 — 16 A3
Park La. TR14 — 17 F4
Park Rd. TR14 — 17 E3
Pavilion Park. TR14 — 17 G1
Pendarves Rd. TR14 — 16 C6
Pendarves St, Beacon. TR14 — 17 G6
Pendarves St, Tuckingmill. TR14 — 17 G1
Pendarves Vw. TR14 — 16 C6
Pendower Ter. TR14 — 17 E6
Pendrea Pk. TR14 — 17 G1
Penforth. TR14 — 17 F5
Pengegon Moor. TR14 — 17 G4
Pengegon Parc. TR14 — 17 G4
Pengegon Way. TR14 — 17 G4
Pengellys Row. TR14 — 17 H1
Pengwarras Rd. TR14 — 16 C3
Penlu. TR14 — 17 H1
Penmorvah Pl. TR14 — 17 F5
Pentalek Rd. TR14 — 17 E5
Penware Parc. TR14 — 17 H1
Primitive Row. TR14 — 17 H1
Primrose Clo. TR14 — 16 B2
Rectory Gdns. TR14 — 16 C4
Rectory Rd. TR14 — 16 C4
Redbrooke Rd. TR14 — 17 E5
Redbrooke Ter. TR14 — 17 E5
Reskadinnick Rd. TR14 — 16 C1
Rock Clo. TR14 — 17 G4
Rose Cotts. TR14 — 17 F3
Roseland Park. TR14 — 16 D1
Rosemellin. TR14 — 17 E1
Rosevale Cres. TR14 — 16 C2
Rosevean Av. TR14 — 17 E3
Rosevean Clo. TR14 — 16 D1
Rosewarne Gdns. TR14 — 16 D3
Rosewarne Mdws. TR14 — 16 D1
Rosewarne Mews. TR14 — 16 D1
Rosewarne Rd. TR14 — 16 D3
Roskear. TR14 — 17 F2
Roskear Fields. TR14 — 17 F2
Roskear Parc. TR14 — 17 F1
Roskear Rd. TR14 — 17 E3
St Martins Clo. TR14 — 16 C4
St Martins Cres. TR14 — 16 C3
St Martins Ter. TR14 — 16 C2
St Meriadoc Rd. TR14 — 16 C2
Sanctuary Clo. TR14 — 16 B4
Sandfield Cres. TR14 — 16 C4
Saras Row. TR14 — 17 E5
Scowbuds. TR14 — 17 G1
Sea View Ter. TR14 — 17 E5
Seton Gdns. TR14 — 16 B2
South Roskear Ter. TR14 — 17 G1
South Ter. TR14 — 16 D5
Stray Park Rd. TR14 — 17 G4
Stray Park Rd. TR14 — 17 E4
Stray Park Way. TR14 — 17 F4
Talveneth. TR14 — 17 G3
Tehidy Rd. TR14 — 16 D1
The Crescent. TR14 — 16 D2
The Glebe. TR14 — 16 C4
Tolcarne Rd. TR14 — 17 G6
Tolcarne St. TR14 — 16 D4
Trecarrack Rd. TR14 — 17 G6
Treen Flats. TR14 — 17 G3

Tregarland Clo. TR14 — 17 F5
Tregenna Ct. TR14 — 16 C5
Tregenna Fields. TR14 — 16 C5
Tregenna La. TR14 — 16 C5
Treglenwith Rd. TR14 — 16 B2
Tregrea. TR14 — 17 F6
Tregurthen Rd. TR14 — 16 C4
Trehane Rd. TR14 — 16 A3
Trelan. TR14 — 17 G3
Trelawney Rd. TR14 — 16 D2
Trelowarren St. TR14 — 16 D3
Tremayne Pk. TR14 — 17 G4
Trenance Rd. TR14 — 17 F1
Trenoweth Av. TR14 — 16 A3
Trenwith Rd. TR14 — 16 B2
Trerise Rd. TR14 — 16 C3
Treswithian Pk Rd. TR14 — 16 A3
Treswithian Rd. TR14 — 16 A3
Trethew Gdns. TR14 — 17 E2
Trevean Clo. TR14 — 16 B3
Trevenson La. TR14 — 16 D4
Trevenson St. TR14 — 16 D3
Trevithick Rd. TR14 — 16 D4
Trevu Rd. TR14 — 16 D4
Uglow Clo. TR14 — 16 C3
Union St. TR14 — 16 D4
Vean Rd. TR14 — 17 E4
Vean Ter. TR14 — 17 E5
Victoria St. TR14 — 16 D4
Vivian Park. TR14 — 17 G5
Vyvyan St. TR14 — 16 D3
Weeth Clo. TR14 — 16 B3
Weeth La. TR14 — 16 B3
Weeth Rd. TR14 — 16 A2
Wellington Clo. TR14 — 16 C3
Wellington Rd. TR14 — 16 D3
Wesley St. TR14 — 17 E3
West Charles St. TR14 — 17 E4
Westborne Rd. TR14 — 16 B2
Wheal Gerry. TR14 — 17 E2
William St. TR14 — 17 E4
Willow Dri. TR14 — 16 B2

CAMELFORD

Anvil Rd. PL32 — 18 B2
Chapel St. PL32 — 18 A2
Clease Meadows. PL32 — 18 A2
Clease Rd. PL32 — 18 A2
College Rd. PL32 — 18 B2
Dark La. PL32 — 18 A2
Daws Meadow. PL32 — 18 C1
Fore St. PL32 — 18 B2
Green Meadows. PL32 — 18 A1
Greenhills. PL32 — 18 A1
High St. PL32 — 18 A3
Higher Cross La. PL32 — 18 C1
Highfield Rd. PL32 — 18 A3
Hillhead Gdns. PL32 — 18 B1
INDUSTRIAL ESTATES:
Highfield Rd Ind Est. PL32 — 18 A3
Llewellyn Clo. PL32 — 18 A3
Longfield Dri. PL32 — 18 A3
Longfield Rd. PL32 — 18 A3
Manor Gdns. PL32 — 18 B2
Market Pl. PL32 — 18 B2
Mill La. PL32 — 18 B1
Mount Camel. PL32 — 18 A2
Penmelen. PL32 — 18 A1
Roughtor Dri. PL32 — 18 A1
Smithy Ct. PL32 — 18 B2
Sportsmans Rd. PL32 — 18 A3
Sunnyside Mdws. PL32 — 18 B1
Trefrew Rd. PL32 — 18 B1
Trevia Lane. PL32 — 18 B1
Tyland Rd. PL32 — 18 D1
Victoria Rd. PL32 — 18 B1
Warrens Field. PL32 — 18 B1

CHARLESTOWN

Appletree La. PL25 — 19 C5
Barkhouse La. PL25 — 19 A6
Beach Rd. PL25 — 19 B5
Boldventure Av. PL25 — 19 A2
Boldventure Clo. PL25 — 19 A2
Boldventure Rd. PL25 — 19 A2

Boscoppa Rd. PL25 — 19 A2
Boscundle Clo. PL25 — 19 C3
Bucklers La. PL25 — 19 A3
Chapel Field. PL25 — 19 A3
Chapel La. PL25 — 19 B1
Charlestown Rd. PL25 — 19 B5
Chatsworth Way. PL25 — 19 B5
Church Rd. PL25 — 19 A5
Crinnis Clo. PL25 — 19 D5
Crinnis Rd. PL25 — 19 A5
Crinnis Wood Av. PL25 — 19 C5
Duporth Rd. PL25 — 19 A6
Edinburgh Clo. PL25 — 19 B5
Fairway. PL25 — 19 C5
Gerrans Clo. PL25 — 19 A2
Gloucester Av. PL25 — 19 B4
Haddon Way. PL25 — 19 B5
Holmbush Arch Rd. PL25 — 19 A4
Holmbush Rd. PL25 — 19 A4
Jubilee Mdw. PL25 — 19 A3
Kent Av. PL25 — 19 C5
Linhay Clo. PL25 — 19 C1
Manfield Way. PL25 — 19 A4
Meadowside. PL25 — 19 B1
Northeast Distributor Rd. PL25 — 19 A1
Oak Tree Clo. PL25 — 19 A4
Par Moor Rd. PL25 — 19 D3
Porthmeor Rd. PL25 — 19 A4
Quay Rd. PL25 — 19 A6
St Austell Rd. PL25 — 19 D3
School La. PL25 — 19 B1
Sea Rd. PL25 — 19 B5
Stennack Rd. PL25 — 19 A4
Trecarne Clo. PL25 — 19 A3
Trenowah Rd. PL25 — 19 A3
Wheal Northy. PL25 — 19 A3
Wheal Regent Pk. PL25 — 19 C5
Windsor Dri. PL25 — 19 B5

FALMOUTH

Acacia Rd. TR11 — 20 B2
Albany Pl. TR11 — 20 D4
Albany Rd. TR11 — 20 D4
Albert Cotts. TR11 — 21 E4
Arundell Grn. TR11 — 20 B2
Arwenack Av. TR11 — 21 E4
Arwenack St. TR11 — 21 E4
Ashfield Estate. TR11 — 20 B2
Ashfield Rd. TR11 — 20 B2
Ashfield Villas. TR11 — 20 B2
Avenue Rd. TR11 — 21 E5
Bar La. TR11 — 21 E5
Bar Rd. TR11 — 21 F5
Bar Ter. TR11 — 21 F4
Bassett Pl. TR11 — 20 D2
Bay Ct. TR11 — 21 E5
Bayview Cres. TR11 — 21 F5
Beacon Cres. TR11 — 20 D3
Beacon Clo. TR11 — 20 D2
Beacon St. TR11 — 20 D2
Beacon Ter. TR11 — 20 D2
Beech Clo. TR11 — 20 C3
Beech Rd. TR11 — 20 C3
Belmont Rd. TR11 — 20 D4
Berkeley Cotts. TR11 — 20 D3
Berkeley Hill. TR11 — 20 D3
*Berkeley Path, Berkeley Hill. TR11 — 20 D3
Berkeley Vale. TR11 — 20 D3
Berryman Cres. TR11 — 20 C5
Bickland Hill. TR11 — 20 A3
Bickland Vale. TR11 — 20 A3
Bickland Water Rd. TR11 — 20 A3
Boscawen Rd. TR11 — 20 D6
Boscundle Av. TR11 — 20 B6
Bosloggas Mews. TR11 — 21 F4
Boslowick Clo. TR11 — 20 B5
Boslowick Rd. TR11 — 20 B6
Bosmeor Clo. TR11 — 20 A5
Bosmeor Rd. TR11 — 20 A5
Bowles Rd. TR11 — 20 C2
Brook Pl. TR11 — 20 D4
Brook Rd. TR11 — 20 C4
Brook St. TR11 — 20 D4
Budock Ter. TR11 — 20 D4
Cambeltown Way. TR11 — 21 E4
Cambridge Pl. TR11 — 20 D5
Captains Walk. TR11 — 20 C5

Carrick Rd. TR11 — 20 B6
Castle Dri. TR11 — 21 G5
Castle Hill. TR11 — 21 F5
Charles Av. TR11 — 20 B5
Chestnut Clo. TR11 — 20 C3
Church St. TR11 — 21 E3
Church Way. TR11 — 20 B4
Clairmont Cotts. TR11 — 20 D3
Clare Ter. TR11 — 21 E4
*Claremont Ter, Beacon St. TR11 — 20 D2
Cliff Rd. TR11 — 21 E5
Clifton Cres. TR11 — 20 D4
Clifton Pl. TR11 — 20 D4
Clifton Ter. TR11 — 20 D4
Colworth Av. TR11 — 20 C4
Conway Rd. TR11 — 20 B3
Conway Gdns. TR11 — 20 A3
Conway Rd. TR11 — 20 A3
Coventry Rd. TR11 — 21 E1
Crossways. TR11 — 20 B6
Daveys Clo. TR11 — 20 B6
De Pass Gdns. TR11 — 21 F5
De Pass Rd. TR11 — 21 F5
Diana Clo. TR11 — 20 B5
Dracaena Av. TR11 — 20 B2
Dracaena Pl. TR11 — 20 C3
Duncannon Dri. TR11 — 20 C4
East Rise. TR11 — 20 C5
Eastwood Rd. TR10 — 20 A4
Elowen Clo. TR11 — 20 A5
Empire Way. TR11 — 20 A4
Emslie Rd. TR11 — 21 E5
Erisey Ter. TR11 — 20 D3
Esperanza Ct. TR11 — 20 C2
Fairfield Rd. TR11 — 20 C3
Falmouth Rd. TR10 — 20 A1
Fawkener Clo. TR11 — 20 B4
Fenwick Rd. TR11 — 20 D5
Ferndale Rd. TR11 — 20 C5
Florence Pl. TR11 — 21 E4
Florence Ter. TR11 — 20 D4
Fox La. TR11 — 21 E4
Foxs La. TR11 — 21 E4
Frankland Clo. TR11 — 20 C4
Freeman Collins Dri. TR11 — 20 B3
Frobisher Ter. TR11 — 20 C5
Frost Ct. TR11 — 20 B3
Garden Mdw. TR11 — 20 B4
Glasney Rd. TR11 — 20 C2
Godolphin Rd. TR11 — 20 C2
Greenbank. TR11 — 20 D2
Grenville Clo. TR11 — 20 C3
Grenville Rd. TR11 — 20 C5
Grove Pl. TR11 — 21 E4
Grovehill Cres. TR11 — 21 E4
Grovehill Dri. TR11 — 21 E5
Gyllyng St. TR11 — 21 E4
Gyllyngvase Hill. TR11 — 21 E5
Gyllyngvase Rd. TR11 — 21 E5
Gyllyngvase Ter. TR11 — 21 E5
Harbour Ter. TR11 — 20 D3
Hawkins Way. TR11 — 20 D4
Hayman Way. TR11 — 20 B2
High St. TR11 — 20 C5
Highfield Rd. TR11 — 20 C5
Hill Head. TR10 — 20 A4
Hillside Meadow. TR10 — 20 A4
Hillside Rd. TR11 — 20 B5
Hulls La. TR11 — 21 E4
INDUSTRIAL & RETAIL:
Tregoniggie Ind Est. TR11 — 20 A4
Jubilee Rd. TR11 — 20 D5
Kelley Rd. TR11 — 20 B3
Kerensa Grn. TR11 — 20 A4
Kersey Rd. TR11 — 21 E4
Killigrew St. TR11 — 20 D4
Kimberley Pk Rd. TR11 — 20 C3
Kimberley Pl. TR11 — 20 C4
Kings Av. TR11 — 20 C5
Laburnum Clo. TR11 — 20 B4
Laburnum Dri. TR11 — 20 B4
Lambs La. TR11 — 20 D5
Langton Rd. TR11 — 20 D4
Langton Ter. TR11 — 20 D4
Lansdowne Rd. TR11 — 21 E5
Link Clo. TR11 — 20 B4
Lister Hill. TR11 — 20 D5
Lister St. TR11 — 20 D5
Longfield. TR11 — 20 B4
Lowenek Clo. TR11 — 20 B4
Madeira Walk. TR11 — 20 D5
Manor Clo. TR11 — 20 A4
Manor Cres. TR11 — 20 A4

Manor Rd. TR11 20 B3
Margaret Pl. TR11 20 C4
Market St. TR11 21 E3
Marlborough Av. TR11 20 C5
Marlborough Clo. TR11 20 C5
Marlborough Ct. TR11 20 C4
Marlborough Cres. TR11 20 C4
Marlborough Gro. TR11 20 C5
Marlborough Rd. TR11 20 D4
Mayfield Rd. TR11 20 C3
Meadowbank Rd. TR11 20 C2
Meadowside Rd. TR11 20 B5
Mearwood La. TR11 20 B3
Melvill Cres. TR11 21 E5
Melvill Rd. TR11 20 D5
Merrill Pl. TR11 20 C1
Messack Clo. TR11 20 B5
Mongleath Av. TR11 20 B4
Mongleath Clo. TR11 20 B5
Mongleath Rd. TR11 20 A4
Mount Stephens La. TR11 20 B3
New St. TR11 21 E4
Norfolk Rd. TR11 20 D4
North Par. TR11 20 C2
Noweth Pl. TR11 20 B2
Oakfield Rd. TR11 20 B2
Old Hill. TR11 20 C2
Old Hill Cres. TR11 20 C2
Packet Quays. TR11 20 D3
Park Cres. TR11 20 C3
Park Hill. TR11 20 D4
Park Rise. TR11 20 C3
Park Ter. TR11 20 C4
Pellew Clo. TR11 20 C2
Pellew Rd. TR11 20 C3
Penarrow Clo. TR11 20 B6
Penarth Rd. TR11 20 D2
Pendarves Rd. TR11 20 C2
Pendennis Rise. TR11 21 F5
Pendennis Rd. TR11 21 F5
Pengarth Rise. TR11 20 C5
Pengarth Rd. TR11 20 C5
Pengelly Pl. TR11 20 B2
Penhale Rd. TR11 20 B6
Penmere Cres. TR11 20 C4
Penmere Hill. TR11 20 C4
Penmere Pl. TR11 20 C4
Pennance Rd. TR11 20 D5
Penrose Rd. TR11 20 C3
Penryn By-Pass. TR11 20 A1
Penvean La. TR11 20 B3
Penwerris La. TR11 20 D2
Penwerris Ter. TR11 20 D2
Pikes Hill. TR11 21 E4
Pit Meadow. TR11 20 B4
Polventon Clo. TR11 20 B3
Polwithen Rd. TR11 20 C3
Porhan Grn. TR11 20 B2
Portland Gdns. TR11 20 C4
Prince St. TR11 20 D3
Prislow Clo. TR11 20 B5
Prislow La. TR11 20 A5
Prislow Fields. TR11 20 B5
*Prospect Pl,
  Beacon St. TR11 20 D2
Quarry Hill. TR11 20 D3
Quay Hill. TR11 21 E4
Queen Anne Gdns. TR11 20 B4
Queen Mary Ct. TR11 20 D6
Queen Mary Rd. TR11 20 D6
Roscarrack Clo. TR11 20 A5
Robert Hichens Rd. TR11 20 C2
St Anthony Way. TR11 20 D5
St Peters Rd. TR11 20 D1
St Smithwick Way. TR11 21 F4
Sea View Rd. TR11 20 D5
Shelburne Rd. TR11 20 B4
Silverdale Rd. TR11 20 D5
Spernen Wyn Rd. TR11 20 D5
Springfield Rd. TR11 20 B3
Stracey Rd. TR11 21 E5
Stratton Ter. TR11 20 D2
Swanpool Hill. TR11 20 D5
Swanpool Rd. TR11 20 C6
Swanpool St. TR11 21 E4
Swanvale Rd. TR11 20 B4
Symons Hill. TR11 20 D2
The Beacon Est. TR11 20 D3

The Causeway. TR11 20 B4
The Gluyas. TR11 20 C4
The Moor. TR11 20 D3
The Nurseries. TR11 20 A3
Theydon Rd. TR11 20 C4
Tinners Walk. TR11 21 F4
Trecarne. TR11 20 B2
Tredova Cres. TR11 20 D6
Tredynas Rd. TR11 21 G5
Tredyson Pl. TR11 20 C4
Trefusis Rd. TR11 20 B6
Trefusis Rd,
  Flushing. TR11 21 E2
Tregenver Rd. TR11 20 C3
Tregenver Villas. TR11 20 C3
Tregoniggie. TR11 20 A3
Tregothan Rd. TR11 20 C3
Tregullow Rd. TR11 20 A3
Tregunter Mews. TR11 21 F4
Trehidy Ter. TR11 20 C1
Trelawney Av. TR11 21 E5
Trelawney Rd. TR11 20 D4
Trelissick Rd. TR11 20 B5
Tremanor Way. TR11 20 A3
Tresahar Rd. TR11 20 D5
Tresawle Rd. TR11 20 C2
Tresawna Ter. TR11 20 D3
Tresco Pl. TR11 20 C3
Trescobeas Rd. TR11 20 A3
Tresillian Rd. TR11 20 C2
Trevarth Rd. TR11 20 B3
Trevaylor Rd. TR11 20 B3
Treveglos Rd. TR11 20 B6
Treventhan Rise. TR11 20 D3
Treventon Clo. TR11 20 B3
Treverbyn Rd. TR11 20 B6
Trevethan Clo. TR11 20 D3
*Trevethan Hill,
  Beacon St. TR11 20 D2
Trevethan Rd. TR11 20 D3
Trevithick Rd. TR11 20 B3
Tuke Clo. TR11 20 B2
Turnaware Rd. TR11 20 B6
Union Corner. TR11 20 A2
Union Rd. TR11 20 A2
Venton Rd. TR11 20 B3
Vernon Pl. TR11 20 D3
Waterloo Rd. TR11 20 D4
Webber St. TR11 20 D3
Weller Ct. TR11 20 D5
Wellington Pl. TR11 20 D4
Wellington Ter. TR11 20 D4
West Rise. TR11 20 B5
West St. TR11 20 D4
Western Ter. TR11 20 D4
Windsor Ct. TR11 20 D4
Windsor Ter. TR11 20 D4
Wodehouse Ter. TR11 21 E4
Wood Clo. TR11 21 E4
Wood Dri. TR11 21 E4
Wood La. TR11 20 D5
Woodlane Cres. TR11 20 D4

FOWEY

Briarfield. PL23 22 C3
Browns Hill. PL23 22 C4
Bull Hill. PL23 22 C4
Cobbs Well. PL23 22 C4
Daglands Rd. PL23 22 B5
Fore St. PL23 22 C4
Fowey Esplanade. PL23 22 A6
Green La. PL23 22 A2
Hanson Dri. PL23 22 A3
Harbour View. PL23 22 C5
Langurtho. PL23 22 A3
Lostwithiel St. PL23 22 C4
Market St. PL23 22 C4
New Road Hill. PL23 22 A3
North St. PL23 22 D3
Park Rd. PL23 22 A3
Passage La. PL23 22 A1
Passage St. PL23 22 D3
Pikes Hill. PL23 22 B5
Place Rd. PL23 22 B4
Rawlings La. PL23 22 C4
Rose Hill. PL23 22 C4
Saffron Clo. PL23 22 B4
St Fimbarrus Rd. PL23 22 A6
South St. PL23 22 C4
Station Rd. PL23 22 C2
Tavern Barn. PL23 22 A2

Town Quay. PL23 22 C4
Vicarage Meadow.
PL23 22 B3
Webb St. PL23 22 C4
Windmill. PL23 22 A3

GUNNISLAKE

Albert Ter. PL18 23 B5
Bealswood Clo. PL18 23 D3
Bealswood Rd. PL18 23 D3
Bedford Clo. PL18 23 B2
Brenton Ter. PL18 23 A6
Calstock Rd. PL18 23 C3
Cemetery Rd. PL18 23 A6
*Chapel Ct,
  Chapel St. PL18 23 C2
Chapel St. PL18 23 B3
Chawleigh Clo. PL18 23 B4
Cliff View Ter. PL18 23 D3
Commercial St. PL18 23 C2
Crockers Row. PL18 23 D3
Crow La. PL18 23 A5
Delaware Clo. PL18 23 A5
Delaware Rd. PL18 23 A3
Drakewells Gdns. PL18 23 B5
Fore St,
  Albaston. PL18 23 A6
Fore St,
  Gunnislake. PL18 23 C2
Gas House La. PL18 23 D3
Hoopers La. PL18 23 B3
King St. PL18 23 B2
Kingswood Rd. PL18 23 C3
Liscombe Clo. PL18 23 C1
Moorland Way. PL18 23 A5
Mudge Ter. PL18 23 C1
New Bridge. PL18 23 C1
Newbridge Hill. PL18 23 C2
Parkers Grn. PL18 23 B2
Pine View. PL18 23 C3
Quarry La. PL18 23 B3
Rodda Clo. PL18 23 C1
Rush Pk. PL18 23 B2
Russell Clo. PL18 23 A3
Sand Hill. PL18 23 B4
Sims Ter. PL18 23 C3
Skinnard La. PL18 23 A6
Star Pk. PL18 23 C2
Station Rd. PL18 23 B5
Stony La. PL18 23 B5
Tamar Ter. PL18 23 C1
Tamar Way. PL18 23 C3
The Crescent. PL18 23 C2
The Orchard. PL18 23 B3
The Paddocks. PL18 23 B5
The Square. PL18 23 C3
Under Rd. PL18 23 C2
Weeks Row. PL18 23 C2
Well Park Rd. PL18 23 B6
Woodland Way. PL18 23 B1

HAYLE

Albertus Dri. TR27 24 A6
Albertus Gdns. TR27 24 A6
Albertus Rd. TR27 24 A6
Baptist Hill. TR27 24 B2
Bay View La. TR27 24 B3
Bay View Ter. TR27 24 D1
Beatrice Ter. TR27 24 D1
Black Rd. TR27 24 C1
Bodriggy Ct. TR27 24 C2
Bodriggy Cres. TR27 24 B3
Bodriggy St. TR27 24 C3
Bodriggy Villas. TR27 24 C3
Boskennal Dri. TR27 24 A6
Bowling Green Ct.
TR27 24 C3
Brookway. TR27 24 D1
Burnthouse La. TR27 24 A4
Carnsew Mdw. TR27 24 A4
Carnsew Rd. TR27 24 A4
Chapel Hill. TR27 24 B3
Chapel La. TR27 24 D2
Chapel Ter. TR27 24 B4
Chy Kensa Clo. TR27 24 C4
Clifton Ter. TR27 24 A2
Commercial Rd. TR27 24 B3
Copper Hill. TR27 24 D2

Copper Ter. TR27 24 D1
Cornubia Clo. TR27 24 C4
Coronation Rd. TR27 24 C4
Crescent Clo. TR27 24 B3
Cross St. TR27 24 B4
Crun Melyn Parc. TR27 24 B4
Curnows Rd. TR27 24 B4
Dracaena Av. TR27 24 D2
Dracaena Cres. TR27 24 D2
East Ter. TR27 24 A3
Ellis Clo. TR27 24 C4
Ellis Way. TR27 24 C3
Fore St. TR27 24 C2
Foundry Hill. TR27 24 A5
Foundry La. TR27 24 A4
Foundry Sq. TR27 24 A4
Glebe Row. TR27 24 C1
Hamilton Clo. TR27 24 B6
Harbour View. TR27 24 B3
Harveys Way. TR27 24 C4
Haven Ct. TR27 24 B4
Hayle By-Pass. TR27 24 C6
Hayle Ter. TR27 24 A3
High Lanes. TR27 24 D3
Higher Church St. TR27 24 A2
Hill Crest Rd. TR27 24 C3
Hollows Ter. TR27 24 D1
Humphry Davy La.
TR27 24 C3
King George V
  Mem Walk. TR27 24 A2
Lethlean La. TR27 24 D1
Lower Church St. TR27 24 C2
Madison Ter. TR27 24 D1
Market Sq. TR27 24 D2
Market St. TR27 24 D2
Mellanear Clo. TR27 24 A6
Mellanear Rd. TR27 24 A6
Millpond Av. TR27 24 A5
Mount Pleasant. TR27 24 B3
Mount Pleasant Gdns.
TR27 24 B3
North Quay. TR27 24 A2
Parc An Dix La. TR27 24 B1
Penpol Av. TR27 24 B4
Penpol Rd. TR27 24 B5
Penpol Ter. TR27 24 A3
Phillack Hill. TR27 24 C1
Polvelyn Parc. TR27 24 A3
Pools Ct. TR27 24 D2
Prospect Pl. TR27 24 D2
Queensway. TR27 24 B4
St Georges Rd. TR27 24 B5
St Johns Ct. TR27 24 C2
St Johns St. TR27 24 C2
St Michaels Clo. TR27 24 A6
Sea La. TR27 24 C2
Springfield Clo. TR27 24 C1
Station Hill. TR27 24 B4
Strawberry La. TR27 24 D6
The Pathway Fields.
TR27 24 B4
Tolview Ter. TR27 24 B5
Trelawney Pl. TR27 24 C3
Trelawney Way. TR27 24 C3
Trelissick Rd. TR27 24 A6
Tremeadow Ter. TR27 24 B3
Tremorva. TR27 24 B3
Trevassack Rd. TR27 24 D2
Trevassack Hill. TR27 24 D2
Treveglos. TR27 24 B3
Trevithick Cres. TR27 24 D4
Trevoarn. TR27 24 A5
West Ter. TR27 24 A3

HELSTON

Albion Rd. TR13 25 B5
Almhouse Hill. TR13 25 A3
Anson Way. TR13 25 D6
Barton Clo. TR13 25 D1
Beacon Clo. TR13 25 C3
Beacon Cres. TR13 25 C3
Beacon Parc. TR13 25 C3
Beacon Ter. TR13 25 C3
Belmont Rd. TR13 25 B1
Bligh Cres. TR13 25 C5
Borlase Clo. TR13 25 B4
Boscawen Rd. TR13 25 D6
Brook Clo. TR13 25 A2
Bullock La. TR13 25 B5
Bulwark Rd. TR13 25 B5
Cades Parc. TR13 25 B3

Canons Pl. TR13 25 D1
Carey Parc. TR13 25 B1
Castel Wary Clo. TR13 25 A4
Casterills Rd. TR13 25 D6
Castle Grn. TR13 25 A3
Champions Ct. TR13 25 A3
Charles Basset Clo.
  TR13 25 C4
Church Hill. TR13 25 B2
Church La. TR13 25 B2
Church St. TR13 25 B2
*Chygothow,
  St Johns Rd. TR13 25 A3
Clodgey La. TR13 25 D2
Clodgey Way. TR13 25 D5
Coinagehall St. TR13 25 B3
Coronation Pl. TR13 25 B5
Cross St. TR13 25 A3
Crosswalla Fields.
  TR13 25 C2
Cunnack Clo. TR13 25 C1
Degibna La. TR13 25 D6
East Clo. TR13 25 D1
Esmonde Rd. TR13 25 D5
Falmouth Rd. TR13 25 D1
Fir Clo. TR13 25 B1
Fitzsimmons Clo. TR13 25 C4
Five Wells La. TR13 25 B3
Furry Walk. TR13 25 B4
Furry Way. TR13 25 B4
Gander La. TR13 25 B3
Glynn Av. TR13 25 B5
Godolphin Rd. TR13 25 C3
Grange Rd. TR13 25 B4
Green Clo. TR13 25 D1
Grenville Rd. TR13 25 D4
Grylls Parc. TR13 25 B2
Gweal Dues. TR13 25 D1
Gwealfolds Rd. TR13 25 C1
Gwealhellis Warren.
  TR13 25 A1
Gwelmeneth. TR13 25 B5
Hawk Rd. TR13 25 D5
Helston Relief Rd.
  TR13 25 A4
Henliston Dri. TR13 25 C5
Hermes Clo. TR13 25 D5
Hermes Rd. TR13 25 C5
Hibernia Rd. TR13 25 D5
Hichens Rd. TR13 25 D5
Higher Well La. TR13 25 C2
Hill Crest. TR13 25 C2
Hill Crest Gdns. TR13 25 C2
Horse & Jockey La.
  TR13 25 C4
Jubilee Ter. TR13 25 C5
Kellaway Park. TR13 25 D3
Kingsley Way. TR13 25 A3
Lady St. TR13 25 A3
*Lanjowan,
  St Johns Rd. TR13 25 A3
Loe Valley Rd TR13 25 A1
Lower Hillcrest. TR13 25 C2
Lower Silver Hill. TR13 25 C2
Lowertown La. TR13 25 B1
Manor Way. TR13 25 D1
Marconi Clo. TR13 25 A2
Meneage Rd. TR13 25 C5
Meneage St. TR13 25 B3
Mill La. TR13 25 A2
Monument Rd. TR13 25 A4
Nans Kestenen. TR13 25 B4
Nansloe Clo. TR13 25 D6
Oates Rd. TR13 25 C3
Olivers Ter. TR13 25 B3
Orchard Clo. TR13 25 A1
Osborne Parc. TR13 25 A2
Parc-an-Dower. TR13 25 C3
Parc Eglos. TR13 25 B2
Parc Leddan. TR13 25 C3
Park Cres. TR13 25 A4
Park View Rd. TR13 25 A4
Pellew Cres. TR13 25 C5
Penberthy Rd. TR13 25 C4
Penhellaz Hill. TR13 25 A3
Penrose Rd. TR13 25 B3
Penventon View. TR13 25 A4
Penview Cres. TR13 25 B4
Penzance Rd. TR13 25 A3
Pine Clo. TR13 25 D4
Porthleven Rd. TR13 25 A4
Prospect Pl. TR13 25 C5
Ratcliffes La. TR13 25 A4
Redruth Rd. TR13 25 D1
Roselidden Parc. TR13 25 B1
Roskilling. TR13 25 D1

Roskilling Wartha.
TR13   25 D1
St Johns Clo. TR13   25 A3
St Johns Rd. TR13   25 A3
Sanctuary La. TR13   25 C3
Seaview Ter. TR13   25 B2
Shute Hill. TR13   25 C3
Station Rd. TR13   25 C1
Tanyard La. TR13   25 C1
Taranto Rd. TR13   25 D5
Tenderah Ct. TR13   25 C2
Tenderah Rd. TR13   25 C2
The Clies. TR13   25 C4
The Paddock. TR13   25 B2
The Parade. TR13   25 C4
Trelawney Rd. TR13   25 C3
Trenethick Way. TR13   25 D1
Trengrouse Way. TR13   25 C3
Trevenen Rd. TR13   25 C3
Trewavas Cres. TR13   24 D4
Troubridge Rd. TR13   25 C5
Turnpike. TR13   25 C1
Tyacke Rd. TR13   25 B4
Vyvyan Pl. TR13   25 C3
Wendron St. TR13   25 B3
West Clo. TR13   25 D1
Winns Row. TR13   25 C2

LAUNCESTON

Angel Hill. PL15   26 C4
Bangors Rd. PL15   26 A6
Bickford Rd. PL15   26 B1
Bounsalls La. PL15   26 C4
Broad Pk. PL15   26 B1
Broad St. PL15   26 C4
Brookside Clo. PL15   26 B1
Bush Park. PL15   26 D5
Castle Dyke. PL15   26 C4
Castle St. PL15   26 B3
Causley Clo. PL15   26 B1
Cemetery La. PL15   26 A5
Chapel Hill. PL15   26 A5
Chapel Park. PL15   26 A5
Church Lea. PL15   26 A2
Church St. PL15   26 C3
College Rd. PL15   26 C6
Cowland Clo. PL15   26 A5
Cross Lanes. PL15   26 C1
Dockacre Ct. PL15   26 C3
Dockacre Rd. PL15   26 C4
Dockey. PL15   26 C4
Duchy Clo. PL15   26 C1
Duke St. PL15   26 A1
Dunheved Fields. PL15   26 B6
Dunheved Rd. PL15   26 B4
Dutson Rd. PL15   26 B2
Exeter Ct. PL15   26 C4
Exeter St. PL15   26 C4
Gendalls Way. PL15   26 B1
George Fox Clo. PL15   26 A5
Hendra Rd. PL15   26 B5
Hendra Vale. PL15   26 B5
High St. PL15   26 C4
Highfield Pk Rd. PL15   26 A5
Hollies Clo. PL15   26 A1
Hollies Rd. PL15   26 A1
Hurdon Rd. PL15   26 C6
Hurdon Way. PL15   26 C6
INDUSTRIAL & RETAIL:
  Newport Ind Est.
  PL15   26 C2
  Pennygillam Ind Est.
  PL15   26 C6
  Scarne Ind Est. PL15   26 C6
Kensey Hill. PL15   26 D4
Landlake Rd. PL15   26 C6
Launceston By-Pass.
  PL15   26 A6
Madford La. PL15   26 C4
Market Ct. PL15   26 C4
Mayne Clo. PL15   26 A2
Meadowside. PL15   26 A5
Moorland Rd. PL15   26 A5
Mount Wise. PL15   26 C4
Newport Sq. PL15   26 B2
North St. PL15   26 A1
Pennygillam Way.
  PL15   26 C6
Penworth Clo. PL15   26 C4
Plestin Clo. PL15   26 C1
Prince Charles Clo.
  PL15   26 C2

Prince Philip Rd. PL15   26 C2
Priory Park Rd. PL15   26 B3
Prouts Clo. PL15   26 C3
Quarry Cres. PL15   26 A6
Queen Elizabeth Rd.
  PL15   26 C2
Race Hill. PL15   26 C4
Ridgegrove Hill. PL15   26 C3
Ridgegrove La. PL15   26 C2
Riverside. PL15   26 B2
Roydon La. PL15   26 B1
Roydon Rd. PL15   26 A1
St Catherines Hill.
  PL15   26 A4
St Cuthbert Clo. PL15   26 A2
St Johns. PL15   26 A5
St Johns Rd. PL15   26 A5
St Josephs Rd. PL15   26 B1
St Leonards Rd. PL15   26 B1
St Marys Rd. PL15   26 C1
St Stephens Hill. PL15   26 A1
St Thomas Hill. PL15   26 B3
St Thomas Rd. PL15   26 B2
Scarne Ind Est. PL15   26 C6
Southgate St. PL15   26 C4
Station Ct. PL15   26 C3
Station Rd. PL15   26 B3
Summerhill Rd. PL15   26 A5
Tavistock Rd. PL15   26 D4
The Cleaves. PL15   26 A1
The Hollies. PL15   26 A1
Tower St. PL15   26 B3
Town Mills. PL15   26 B3
Trecarn Clo. PL15   26 A5
Trecarrell. PL15   26 C5
Tredydan Rd. PL15   26 B3
Trelawney. PL15   26 D4
Trevallyn Rd. PL15   26 B6
Underhayes La. PL15   26 A1
Underlane. PL15   26 A3
Westbridge Rd. PL15   26 B2
Western Rd. PL15   26 B5
*Westgate Mews,
  Dockey. PL15   26 C4
Westgate St. PL15   26 B4
Windmill Hill. PL15   26 C4
Windmill La. PL15   26 C4
Woburn Rd. PL15   26 B5
Wooda La. PL15   26 B3
Wooda Rd. PL15   26 B3

LELANT

Abbey Hill. TR26   27 A1
Abbey Meadows. TR26   27 B1
Brewery Hill. TR26   27 C3
Brush End. TR26   27 B1
Church Clo. TR26   27 C2
Church La. TR26   27 D3
Church Rd. TR26   27 C2
Estuary Vw. TR26   27 B2
Fairfield Clo. TR26   27 C3
Fore St. TR26   27 B1
Green La. TR26   27 C3
Lelant Mdws. TR26   27 C2
Mount Pleasant. TR26   27 B1
Riverside. TR26   27 B2
St Uny Clo. TR26   27 B2
Saltings Clo. TR26   27 B2
Station Hill. TR26   27 C3
The Saltings. TR26   27 A1
Trendreath Clo. TR26   27 C2
Tyringham Rd. TR26   27 C2
Vicarage La. TR26   27 B2

LISKEARD

Allen Vale. PL14   28 B4
Ashbury Clo. PL14   29 F2
Barn St. PL14   29 E4
Barras Cross. PL14   29 E3
Barras Pl. PL14   29 E3
Barras St. PL14   29 E4
Baytree Hill. PL14   29 E4
Beech Av. PL14   28 D5
Bodgara Way. PL14   29 F4
Bonython Ter. PL14   28 D6
Boveway Dri. PL14   29 G4
Boveway La. PL14   29 G4

Bowling Green Ct.
  PL14   28 D4
Briarwood. PL14   29 G4
Brisbane Ter. PL14   28 D5
Buller Pk. PL14   29 G5
Callington Rd. PL14   29 E3
Cannon Hill. PL14   29 F2
Cannon Ter. PL14   29 E4
Caradon Dri. PL14   28 D3
Caradon Heights. PL14   29 G2
Carthew Clo. PL14   29 G4
Castle Hill. PL14   29 E4
Castle La. PL14   29 E4
Castle St. PL14   29 F4
Church Gate. PL14   29 F4
Church Pl. PL14   29 E4
Church St. PL14   29 E4
Charter Way. PL14   29 H2
Church St North. PL14   29 F4
Church St South. PL14   29 F4
Clemo Rd. PL14   29 H2
Coldstyle Rd. PL14   29 E2
Connoc Clo. PL14   29 G4
Courtney Rd. PL14   29 G3
Crabtree Clo. PL14   28 D5
Culverland Pk. PL14   29 E1
Culverwood Rd. PL14   29 E1
Dark La. PL14   29 F2
Dean Hill. PL14   28 D3
Dean La. PL14   28 D3
Dean St. PL14   28 D4
Dennis Rd. PL14   29 F2
Doctors La. PL14   29 E3
Donierts Clo. PL14   28 D4
Dungarth Grn. PL14   29 F4
Dungarth Rd. PL14   29 F4
Eastern Av. PL14   29 G2
Eddystone Rise. PL14   29 G2
Evely Ct. PL14   29 F2
Fair Park Rd. PL14   29 E4
Fore St. PL14   29 E4
Gaunter Rd. PL14   29 G4
Gipsy La. PL14   28 B4
Glynn Rd. PL14   28 B4
Greenbank La. PL14   29 E3
Greenbank Rd. PL14   29 E3
Grove Dri. PL14   28 B4
Grove Park Ct. PL14   28 D6
Hanson Rd. PL14   29 G3
Hazelmead. PL14   28 D5
Heathlands La. PL14   29 E5
Heathlands Rd. PL14   28 D5
Henfordh Grange. PL14   28 C3
Henscol Vale. PL14   28 C4
Herring Clo. PL14   29 G2
Herring La. PL14   29 G2
Higher Lux St. PL14   29 E3
Holman Rd. PL14   29 H2
INDUSTRIAL & RETAIL:
  Caradon Business Pk.
  PL14   29 E5
  Heathlands Ind Est.
  PL14   29 E5
  Miller Business Pk.
  PL14   28 D6
  Moorswater Ind Est.
  PL14   28 A5
  Oaklands Ind Est.
  PL14   29 H2
Jack Bice Clo. PL14   29 H4
Killigrew Rd. PL14   29 F4
Kilmar Rd. PL14   29 H2
Lake Lane. PL14   29 F4
Lanchard La. PL14   28 C5
Lanchard Rise. PL14   28 C4
Lanchard Rd. PL14   28 D4
Lang Rd. PL14   28 D6
Lawry Clo. PL14   28 D5
Limes La. PL14   28 C4
Liskerret Rd. PL14   29 G5
Little Dean. PL14   28 D3
Lower Lux St. PL14   29 E3
Lux Cross. PL14   29 F2
Luxstowe Dri. PL14   29 F3
Maddever Cres. PL14   29 F4
Manley Clo. PL14   28 C5
Manley Ter. PL14   28 D5
Market App. PL14   29 E4
Market St. PL14   29 E4
Martins Clo. PL14   29 H2
Maudlin Clo. PL14   28 D5
Meadow Pk. PL14   28 D5
Melbourne Rd. PL14   29 F4
Miners Way. PL14   29 G2
Moorland Clo. PL14   29 F2

Moorland View.
  PL14   29 F2
New Rd. PL14   28 B5
Oak Dri. PL14   28 D5
Oaklands Rd. PL14   29 H3
Old Rd. PL14   28 A4
Old Station Rd. PL14   28 A5
Park Fenton. PL14   29 G4
Park Rd. PL14   29 F3
Park View. PL14   29 F3
Passmore Clo. PL14   29 G4
Pavlova Ct. PL14   29 E5
Pendean Av. PL14   28 D3
Pendean Clo. PL14   28 D3
Pendean Ct. PL14   28 D3
Pendean Dri. PL14   28 D3
Pendragon Rd. PL14   29 F4
Pengover Clo. PL14   29 F3
Pengover Heights.
  PL14   29 G3
Pengover Pk. PL14   29 F3
Pengover Rd. PL14   29 F2
Peppers Park Rd. PL14   29 H3
Pigmeadow La. PL14   29 E4
Pike St. PL14   29 E3
Plymouth Rd. PL14   29 F4
Poldhu Rd. PL14   29 G4
Pond Br Hill. PL14   29 E4
Portland Clo. PL14   29 F2
Portland Ter. PL14   29 F2
Pound Dean. PL14   28 C5
Pound St. PL14   29 E3
Putnam Clo. PL14   29 F5
Quimperle Way. PL14   29 H3
Rapson Rd. PL14   29 G3
Respryn Clo. PL14   29 G2
Rosemellen Ter. PL14   28 D6
Rundle Ct. PL14   28 D6
Russell St. PL14   29 E5
St Cleer Rd. PL14   29 F1
Samuel Bone Clo.
  PL14   29 G3
Silvanus Jenkin Av.
  PL14   29 H5
Smiths Cotss. PL14   29 F3
Springfield Rd. PL14   29 G3
Spurway Rd. PL14   29 F4
Stanley Maggs Way.
  PL14   29 H5
Station Rd. PL14   28 D6
Stephens Rd. PL14   29 H2
Sun Girt La. PL14   29 E4
The Crescent. PL14   29 E3
The Parade. PL14   29 E3
Thorn Pk. PL14   28 D4
Tollgate Clo. PL14   28 D6
Tom Lyon Rd. PL14   29 H5
Tregartha Way. PL14   29 G2
Tregay La. PL14   29 F1
Tremeddan Ct. PL14   29 E3
Tremeddan La. PL14   29 E3
Tremeddan Ter. PL14   28 D6
Trevanion Rd. PL14   29 F5
Treverbyn Clo. PL14   29 H2
Trevillis Pk. PL14   28 D6
Turnpike Pl. PL14   28 D6
Varley La. PL14   28 D4
Venslooe Hill. PL14   28 D1
Victoria Clo. PL14   29 E3
Wadeland Ter. PL14   28 B5
Wadham Clo. PL14   29 F4
Wadham Dri. PL14   29 F4
Wadham Rd. PL14   29 F5
Well La. PL14   29 E4
West St. PL14   28 D3
Westbourne La. PL14   29 E3
Western Av. PL14   28 B4
Westwood. PL14   28 D3
Whitley Grange. PL14   28 C3
William Young Mews.
  PL14   29 H5
Willow Way. PL14   28 C5
Windsor Pl. PL14   29 E4
Woodgate Rd. PL14   28 B4
Wrey Av. PL14   29 E1
Yeomans Clo. PL14   29 F4

LOOE

Barbican Clo. PL13   30 C3
Barbican Hill. PL13   30 C3
Barbican Rd. PL13   30 C3
Bay Down. PL13   30 D2
Bay View Dri. PL13   30 D3

Bay View Rd. PL13   30 C3
Beech Ter. PL13   30 A3
Bodrigan Rd. PL13   30 C2
Buller St. PL13   30 B5
Castle St. PL13   30 B4
Chantry La. PL13   30 D3
Chapel Ground. PL13   30 A5
Church St. PL13   30 B5
Churchlands. PL13   30 C1
Cleveland Av. PL13   30 C3
Courtenay Clo. PL13   30 C3
Darloe La. PL13   30 A4
Dawes La. PL13   30 C2
Dawn Rd. PL13   30 B5
Downs Rd. PL13   30 A5
Downs Vw. PL13   30 A5
East Cliff. PL13   30 C4
Elm Tree Rd. PL13   30 B3
Fairfields. PL13   30 C2
Fore St, E. Looe. PL13   30 B4
Fore St, W. Looe. PL13   30 A5
Glebelands. PL13   30 C1
Goonrea. PL13   30 A4
Goonwartha Rd. PL13   30 A4
Hannafore La. PL13   30 B5
Hannafore Rd. PL13   30 B5
Hay La. PL13   30 C3
Higher Market St. PL13   30 B4
INDUSTRIAL & RETAIL:
  Barbican Rise Workshop
  Units PL13   30 D3
Listowel Dri. PL13   30 D3
Lower St. PL13   30 B5
Marine Dri. PL13   30 C6
Meadow Dri. PL13   30 D2
Meadway. PL13   30 C3
Middle Market St. PL13   30 B4
North Rd. PL13   30 B4
North View. PL13   30 B2
Penarth. PL13   30 A4
Pendennis Rd. PL13   30 C2
Pendower Rd. PL13   30 D3
Pendrim Rd. PL13   30 B3
Plaidy La. PL13   30 D3
Plaidy Park Rd. PL13   30 D3
Polperro Rd. PL13   30 A3
Polvellan Ter. PL13   30 A3
Portbyhan Rd. PL13   30 A4
Portuan Rd. PL13   30 B6
Princes St. PL13   30 B4
Princess Sq. PL13   30 B5
Quay Rd. PL13   30 B4
Rame Vw. PL13   30 C3
Restormel Rd. PL13   30 C3
St Georges Rd. PL13   30 C3
St Martins Clo. PL13   30 C1
St Martins Rd. PL13   30 B1
St Winnols Pk. PL13   30 C3
Sandplace Rd. PL13   30 B1
Shutta. PL13   30 B2
Shutta Hill. PL13   30 B2
Springfield Rd. PL13   30 C2
Station Rd. PL13   30 B3
Sunrising Est. PL13   30 C1
The Downs. PL13   30 A3
Trenant Rd. PL13   30 C2
Trewint Cres. PL13   30 C2
Well La. PL13   30 A5
West Looe Hill. PL13   30 A5
West Rd. PL13   30 A3
Woodlands Vw. PL13   30 A3

LOSTWITHIEL

Albert Ter. PL22   31 B3
Barn Park. PL22   31 D3
Bodmin Hill. PL22   31 A1
Butts Park. PL22   31 D2
Carbes La. PL22   31 B2
Castle Hill. PL22   31 A3
Church La. PL22   31 B2
Clifden Ter. PL22   31 B1
Coffa Bridge Clo. PL22   31 C1
Coffeelake Meadow.
  PL22   31 D3
Cott Rd. PL22   31 C2
Couchwell La. PL22   31 A4
Dark La. PL22   31 B1
Duke St. PL22   31 B1
Edgcumbe Rd. PL22   31 A1
Fore St. PL22   31 B1
Fortescue Pl. PL22   31 D1

Glenworth Ter. PL22 31 B1
Grenville Mdws. PL22 31 D2
Grenville Rd. PL22 31 C2
Guildhall La. PL22 31 B2
Hillside Gdns. PL22 31 B2
King St. PL22 31 B3
Knights Ct. PL22 31 A1
Lanwithan Clo. PL22 31 D2
Lanwithan Rd. PL22 31 D2
Liddicoat Rd. PL22 31 B1
Malthouse La. PL22 31 B2
Meadow Breeze. PL22 31 A2
Melville Ter. PL22 31 B1
Mill Gdns. PL22 31 B2
Mill Hill. PL22 31 C2
Millham La. PL22 31 D1
Monmouth La. PL22 31 B2
Monmouth Ter. PL22 31 B2
Mount Pleasant. PL22 31 A1
North St. PL22 31 B2
Old Grammar
  School Ct. PL22 31 B2
Park Rd. PL22 31 B3
Peckneck Ter. PL22 31 B3
Pendour Park. PL22 31 D1
Pill La. PL22 31 B3
Pleyberchrist Way.
  PL22 31 B1
Quay St. PL22 31 B3
Queen St. PL22 31 B2
Reeds Park. PL22 31 D2
Restormel Estates.
  PL22 31 C1
Restormel Rd. PL22 31 B2
Riverside. PL22 31 B2
Robartes Ter. PL22 31 A1
Rose Hill Clo. PL22 31 A2
Rosehill. PL22 31 A3
St Georges Park. PL22 31 A1
St Nicholas Park. PL22 31 A1
Scrations La. PL22 31 A2
Shute Hill. PL22 31 B2
Skiddery Hill. PL22 31 B3
South St. PL22 31 B2
Springfield Clo. PL22 31 C2
Summers St. PL22 31 B2
Tanhouse Rd. PL22 31 A1
Terras Hill. PL22 31 B2
The Moors. PL22 31 B2
The Parade. PL22 31 B2
The Terrace. PL22 31 A2
Trewince La. PL22 31 A1
Trewithan Park. PL22 31 D2
Uzella Park. PL22 31 A1

MARAZION

Back La. TR17 32 C2
Beacon Rd. TR17 32 C2
Boltern Rd. TR17 32 E2
Chapel St. TR17 32 C2
Churchway. TR17 32 E2
Cormoran Ct. TR17 32 E2
East Cliff La. TR17 32 D2
Eliskirk La. TR17 32 B1
Fore St. TR17 32 C2
Forreglos Dri. TR17 32 E2
Godolphin Av. TR17 32 B1
Godolphin Dri. TR17 32 B2
Godolphin Pl. TR17 32 B2
Godolphin Ter. TR17 32 B1
Green La. TR17 32 D2
Swallon La. TR17 32 D2
Swel An Mor. TR17 32 C2
Henfor Clo. TR17 32 E2
Henfor Ter. TR17 32 E2
Higher Fore St. TR17 32 D2
Kings La. TR17 32 C2
Keys La. TR17 32 C2
Malthouse La. TR17 32 C2
Market Pl. TR17 32 E2
Millet Clo. TR17 32 E2
Mount View Ter. TR17 32 E2
Oates Rd. TR17 32 B2
Old Smithy Clo. TR17 32 E2
Plain-An-Gwarry La.
  TR17 32 E2
Praeds La. TR17 32 C2
Rose Hill. TR17 32 C1
St Levan Clo. TR17 32 E2
St Levan Rd. TR17 32 E2
School La. TR17 32 D2

Shop Hill. TR17 32 D2
The Causeway. TR17 32 B3
The Square. TR17 32 C2
Trevenner La. TR17 32 E2
Trevenner Sq. TR17 32 D2
Treworvenneth Dri.
  TR17 32 E2
Turnpike Hill. TR17 32 C2
Turnpike Rd. TR17 32 D2
West End. TR17 32 B2
Wheal-An-Wens. TR17 32 D2
Woolcocke Clo. TR17 32 E2

MEVAGISSEY

Battery Ter. PL26 31 C5
Beach Rd. PL26 31 C4
Chapel Sq. PL26 31 C5
Chapel St. PL26 31 C5
Church La. PL26 31 B4
Church St. PL26 31 C5
Cliff Rd. PL26 31 C4
Cliff St. PL26 31 C5
Crosspark Ter. PL26 31 C4
*Du Maurier Ct,
  Fore St. PL26 31 C5
East Quay. PL26 31 C5
East Wharf. PL26 31 C5
Fore St. PL26 31 C5
Higher Lavorrick. PL26 31 C4
Higher Well Park. PL26 31 C4
Jetty St. PL26 31 C5
Kiln Clo. PL26 31 C4
Lamorak Clo. PL26 31 B5
Lavorrick Orchards
  PL26 31 C4
Lower Well Park. PL26 31 C4
Market Sq. PL26 31 C5
Mount St. PL26 31 C5
Olivers Quay. PL26 31 C5
Penmeva View. PL26 31 B5
Pentillie. PL26 31 C5
Pentillie Way. PL26 31 C6
Penwarne La. PL26 31 C6
Polkirt Hill. PL26 31 C6
Polkirk Mews. PL26 31 C5
Portmellon Hill. PL26 31 C6
Portmellon Park. PL26 31 C6
Prospect Pl. PL26 31 C5
Prospect Ter. PL26 31 C5
*Rebecca Ct,
  River St. PL26 31 B5
*St George Sq,
  Church St. PL26 31 C5
School Hill. PL26 31 C4
Summerfield Clo. PL26 31 B5
*The Meadows,
  Fore St. PL26 31 C5
Tregony Hill. PL26 31 B5
Trevarth. PL26 31 B5
Valley Park. PL26 31 C5
Valley Rd. PL26 31 B4
Vicarage Hill. PL26 31 B4
*Wesley Ct,
  Fore St. PL26 31 C5
West Quay. PL26 31 C5

MILLBROOK/ KINGSAND

Anderton Rise. PL10 33 B3
Armada Rd. PL10 33 C6
Barton Mews. PL10 33 B1
Blindwell Hill. PL10 33 B2
Calvez Clo. PL10 33 C1
Camperknowle Clo.
  PL10 33 C1
Cawsand Park. PL10 33 C5
Coombe La. PL10 33 C5
Coombe Park Clo. PL10 33 C5
Devonport Hill. PL10 33 D5
Earles Rd. PL10 33 D5
Edgcumbe Cres. PL10 33 C1
Egret Clo. PL10 33 C1
Forder Hill. PL10 33 B6
Forder La. PL10 33 C6
Fore St,
  Kingsand. PL10 33 D5
Fore St,
  Millbrook. PL10 33 B2

Garrett St. PL10 33 D6
Green Pk. PL10 33 C5
Greenland. PL10 33 B2
Hat La. PL10 33 B6
Heavitree Rd. PL10 33 D5
Heron Clo. PL10 33 C1
Higher Anderton Rd.
  PL10 33 B2
Hounster Dri. PL10 33 A3
Insworke Clo. PL10 33 C1
Insworke Cres. PL10 33 C1
Insworke Pl. PL10 33 C1
Jackmans Mdw. PL10 33 C4
King St. PL10 33 B2
Knill Cross. PL10 33 B2
Little La. PL10 33 D5
Little Point Cres. PL10 33 C2
Lower Anderton Rd.
  PL10 33 B2
Lower Row. PL10 33 D5
Maker La. PL10 33 B2
Market St. PL10 33 D6
Millpool Head. PL10 33 B2
Millpool Rd. PL10 33 C1
Millview Gdns. PL10 33 B2
Millview Rd. PL10 33 B2
Molesworth Ter. PL10 33 C6
New Rd. PL10 33 C6
New Rd Clo. PL10 33 C5
New St. PL10 33 B2
Newport St. PL10 33 B2
Radford La. PL10 33 A3
St Andrews Pl. PL10 33 C6
St Andrews St,
  Cawsand. PL10 33 C6
St Andrews St,
  Millbrook. PL10 33 A2
St Johns Clo. PL10 33 B2
St Johns Rd. PL10 33 A1
Sango Ct. PL10 33 C5
Southdown Rd. PL10 33 C1
Speedwell Clo. PL10 33 B2
The Cleave. PL10 33 D5
The Drive. PL10 33 D5
The Green. PL10 33 D5
The Parade. PL10 33 B2
The Square. PL10 33 D6
Trencher La. PL10 33 A5
Wells Ct. PL10 33 A3
Welman Rd. PL10 33 C1
West St. PL10 33 A3
Woodcock Clo. PL10 33 C1

NEWQUAY

Acland Gdns. TR7 34 B3
Agar Rd. TR7 34 C4
Albany Rd. TR7 34 D3
Alexandra Ct. TR7 35 F2
Alexandra Rd. TR7 35 F2
Alldritt Clo. TR7 35 H3
Alma Pl. TR7 34 B3
Anthony Rd. TR7 34 B5
Arundel Way. TR7 35 E2
Atlantic Rd. TR7 34 A4
Aylwin Clo. TR7 35 H3
Bank St. TR7 34 B4
Bay View Ter. TR7 34 B4
Beach Rd,
  Newquay. TR7 34 B3
Beach Rd, Porth. TR7 35 F2
Beachfield Av. TR7 34 B3
Beacon Rd. TR7 34 B3
Bedowan Mdws. TR7 35 E5
Belmont Pl. TR7 34 B3
Berry Rd. TR7 34 C4
Billings Dri. TR7 35 E5
Bolowthas Way. TR7 35 F2
Bonython Rd. TR7 35 E5
Bosuen Way. TR7 35 E5
Bothwicks Rd. TR7 34 B4
Bracken Ter. TR7 34 C4
Bradley Rd. TR7 35 E5
Bramble Clo. TR7 35 E5
Bridge Clo. TR7 35 E6
*Broad St,
  Alma Pl. TR7 34 B3
Calshot Clo. TR7 35 H3
Carclew Av. TR7 34 C4
Cardell Way. TR7 35 E4
Carminow Way. TR7 35 E2
Carmython St. TR7 34 C4
Carpmael Av. TR8 35 F5

Carter Clo. TR7 35 E5
*Central Sq,
  Fore St. TR7 34 B4
Century Ct. TR7 35 G2
*Chapel Hill,
  Fore St. TR7 34 B3
Chapel Rd. TR8 35 H6
Cheltenham Pl. TR7 34 B4
Chester Rd. TR7 35 E3
Cheviot Rd. TR7 34 C5
Chichester Cres. TR7 34 D5
Christian Way. TR7 35 G2
Church La. TR7 35 H2
Church St. TR7 35 H3
Chylan Cres. TR7 35 H2
Chynance Dri. TR7 34 B5
Chyverton Clo. TR7 34 B5
Clemens Clo. TR7 35 E5
Clevedon Rd. TR7 34 B4
Clifden Clo. TR7 34 C4
Cliff Rd. TR7 34 C3
Colvreath Rd. TR7 34 D3
Coronation Way. TR7 35 G2
Crantock St. TR7 34 A4
Cross Clo. TR7 35 G2
Crown Clo. TR7 34 D5
Curlew Clo. TR7 34 A4
Dale Clo. TR7 34 D6
Dale Rd. TR7 35 E6
Dane Rd. TR7 34 C5
Downside Clo. TR7 35 E5
Duchy Av. TR7 35 G3
Dukes Way. TR7 35 E4
Earls Rise. TR7 35 E4
East St. TR7 34 C4
Edgcumbe Av. TR7 34 D3
Edgcumbe Gdns. TR7 34 D3
Eliot Gdns. TR7 34 D3
Elm Clo. TR7 34 D6
Ennors Rd. TR7 34 B4
Estuary Vw. TR7 34 B5
Fairview Ter. TR7 34 C4
Felixstowe Clo. TR7 35 H3
Fernhill Rd. TR7 34 B3
Fore St. TR7 34 B3
Gannel Rd. TR7 34 A4
Gannel View Clo. TR7 35 F6
Glamis Rd. TR7 35 E3
Godolphin Way. TR7 35 F2
Golf Ter. TR7 34 A3
Goonvrea Clo. TR7 34 D5
Gorse Clo. TR7 35 E5
Gover La. TR7 34 B4
Greenbank Cres. TR7 35 G2
Gresham Clo. TR7 34 D5
Grosvenor Av. TR7 34 C4
Hawkins Rd. TR7 34 C4
Headland Rd. TR7 34 A2
Headleigh Rd. TR7 34 C4
Henver Rd. TR7 35 E3
Henwood Cres. TR7 35 H3
Higher Tower Rd. TR7 34 A4
Higher Well Clo. TR7 35 E5
Hilgrove Rd. TR7 34 D3
Holywell Rd. TR7 34 D4
Hope Ter. TR7 34 B3

INDUSTRIAL & RETAIL:
Treloggan Ind Est.
  TR7 35 E6
Island Cres. TR7 34 C3
Jubilee St. TR7 34 B4
Kew Clo. TR7 34 D5
*Killacourt,
  Town Prom. TR7 34 B3
King Edward Cres. TR7 34 B2
*King St,
  Fore St. TR7 34 B4
Kingsley Mead. TR7 35 F5
Lanhenvor Av. TR7 34 C4
Leader Rd. TR7 35 E4
Lewarne Cres. TR7 35 G2
Lewarne Rd. TR7 35 G2
Linden Av. TR7 34 C5
Linden Cres. TR7 34 C5
Listry Rd. TR7 34 C5
Little Down Pk. TR7 35 E6
Lusty Glaze Rd. TR7 35 E6
Manewas Way. TR7 35 E6
Manor Rd. TR7 34 B4
Marcus Hill. TR7 34 B4
Mayfield Cres. TR7 34 C4
Mayfield Rd. TR7 34 C4
Meadow Clo. TR7 34 D5
Meadowside. TR7 34 D5
Mellanvrane La. TR7 34 D5
Michell Av. TR7 34 C4

Middleton Cres. TR7 34 D5
Mount Wise. TR7 34 B4
Mountbatten Clo. TR7 35 H2
Mow Hay Clo. TR7 35 E5
Narrowcliff. TR7 34 D3
Nathan Clo. TR7 35 F4
North Quay Hill. TR7 34 B3
Oakleigh Ter. TR7 34 C3
Old Barn Clo. TR7 34 B5
Parc Godrevy. TR7 34 A4
Pargolla Rd. TR7 34 C4
Parkenbutts. TR7 35 H2
Parkland Clo. TR7 35 H3
Pembroke Rd. TR7 35 H3
Pendragon Cres. TR7 35 E6
Pengannel Clo. TR7 34 B5
Penhallow Rd. TR7 35 F2
Penina Av. TR7 34 D6
Penmere Dri. TR7 34 A4
Penmerrin Cres. TR7 34 C4
Pentire Rd. TR7 34 A4
Penwartha Clo. TR7 35 G3
Place Parc. TR7 35 H2
Polwhele Rd. TR7 35 E6
Porth Bean Rd. TR7 35 F2
Porth Par. TR7 35 F2
Porth Way. TR7 35 F3
Praze Rd. TR7 35 F2
Priory Rd. TR7 35 H2
Pydar Clo. TR7 35 F4
Quarry Park Rd. TR7 34 D4
Quintrell Rd. TR7 34 D4
Rawley La. TR7 34 C5
Reeds Way. TR7 34 B4
Rialton Heights. TR7 35 H2
Rialton Rd. TR7 35 H3
Robartes Rd. TR7 34 C5
Roma Ct. TR7 35 G3
St Annes Rd. TR7 34 D3
St Aubyn Cres. TR7 35 E3
St Cuthberts Rd. TR7 34 B4
St Georges Rd. TR7 34 B4
St Johns Rd. TR7 34 B4
St Marys Rd. TR7 34 B4
St Michaels Rd. TR7 34 B4
St Pirans Rd. TR7 34 A4
St Thomas Rd. TR7 34 C4
School Clo. TR7 35 H3
Seymour Av. TR7 34 C5
Shackleton Dri. TR7 35 E4
South Quay Hill. TR7 34 B3
Springfield Rd. TR7 34 C4
Stafford Rd. TR7 35 G3
Stanharver Clo. TR7 35 H3
Stanways Rd. TR7 35 H2
Station App. TR7 34 D3
Station Par. TR7 34 D3
Sweet Briar Cres. TR7 35 E5
Sydney Rd. TR7 34 B3
Tamarisk La. TR7 34 D5
The Crescent. TR7 34 B3
Toby Way. TR7 34 D4
Tolcarne Mews. TR7 34 D4
Tolcarne Rd. TR7 34 C4
Tor Rd. TR7 34 C4
Towan Blystra Rd. TR7 35 E4
Tower Rd. TR7 34 A3
Town Promenade. TR7 34 B3
Trebarwith Cres. TR7 34 C3
Tredour Rd. TR7 34 C5
Treforda Rd. TR7 34 D5
Trefry Ct. TR7 34 B4
Tregoss Rd. TR7 34 D3
Tregunnel Hill. TR7 34 B5
Trelawney Rd. TR7 34 D5
Treloggan La. TR7 34 D5
Treloggan Rd. TR7 34 D5
Trembath Cres. TR7 34 C5
Trenance La. TR7 34 C5
Trenance Rd. TR7 34 C5
Trenarth Rd. TR7 34 C4
Trencreek La. TR8 35 F5
Trencreek Rd. TR8 35 F5
Treninnick Hill. TR7 34 D5
Trerice Dri. TR7 35 E4
Trethellan Hill. TR7 34 A4
Tretherras Clo. TR7 35 E4
Tretherras Rd. TR7 34 D4
Trethewey Way. TR7 34 B5
Trevan Way. TR7 34 A4
Trevelgue Rd. TR7 35 F1
Trevemper Rd. TR7 34 C5
Trevena Ter. TR7 34 B3
Trevenson Rd. TR7 35 F4
Treviglas Clo. TR7 35 G3

arade St. TR18 38 E4
arc Letta. TR18 38 B2
arc Mellan. TR18 38 D2
arc Wartha Av. TR18 38 D3
arc Wartha Cres. TR18 38 D3
ark Corner. TR18 38 D4
ark Rd. TR18 39 B7
ark Ter. TR18 39 B7
enalverne Av. TR18 38 D4
enalverne Cres. TR18 38 D4
enalverne Dri. TR18 38 D4
enalverne Pl. TR18 38 D4
enare Rd. TR18 38 E3
enare Ter. TR18 38 E3
enarwyn Cres. TR18 38 B2
enbrea Rd. TR18 38 D2
endarves Rd. TR18 38 D3
endennis Clo. TR18 38 E2
endennis Pl. TR18 38 E2
endennis Rd. TR18 38 E2
endrea Clo. TR18 38 F2
endrea Pl. TR18 38 F2
endrea Rd. TR18 38 F2
engwell. TR18 39 B6
enlee Manor Dri. TR18 39 D5
enlee St. TR18 38 E3
enlee View Ter. TR18 39 D5
enmere Clo. TR18 38 D2
enmere Pl. TR18 38 D2
enmere Rd. TR18 38 D2
enpons Clo. TR18 39 C5
enrose Gdns. TR18 38 E3
enrose Ter. TR18 38 E3
enwith St. TR18 38 E3
enzance By-Pass. TR18 38 B4
everell Rd. TR18 38 E3
ine Rd. TR18 39 B5
olgarth. TR18 39 B6
olglaze Clo. TR18 38 D2
olgoon Clo. TR18 38 C4
olmeere Rd. TR18 38 D2
olmennor Rd. TR18 38 C2
oltair Clo. TR18 38 B2
oltair Ter. TR18 38 B2
olventon Clo. TR18 38 B2
olweath Rd. TR18 38 D2
olwithen Rd. TR18 38 C4
olwyn Clo. TR18 38 B2
ortreath Clo. TR18 38 D2
rinces St. TR18 38 E4
romenade. TR18 39 D5
rovis Rd. TR18 39 C5
uay St. TR18 38 E4
ueen St. TR18 38 E4
uillet Rd. TR18 39 B6
edinnick Gdns. TR18 39 D5
edinnick Pl. TR18 39 D5
edinnick Ter. TR18 39 D5
eens Cres. TR18 38 C2
eens Rd. TR18 38 C2
egent Sq. TR18 38 E4
egent Ter. TR18 39 E5
estormel Rd. TR18 39 B6
ichmond St. TR18 38 D3
ichmond St, Heamoor. TR18 38 C2
idgevale Clo. TR18 38 F1
idgevale La. TR18 38 F1
ock Rd. TR18 39 C6
ock Ter. TR18 39 C2
ope Walk. TR18 39 B5
oscadghill Parc. TR18 38 B3
oscadghill Rd. TR18 38 B3
osehill Gdns. TR18 38 B3
osehill Mdw. TR18 38 B3
oseparvah Gdns 38 B2
osevale. TR18 39 D5
osevean Rd. TR18 38 E3
osevean Ter. TR18 38 D3
St Clare St. TR18 38 D3
St Clare Ter. TR18 38 D3
*St Francis St, Barwis Hill. TR18 38 E3
St Golder Rd. TR18 39 B6
St Henry St. TR18 38 E3
St James St. TR18 38 E4
St Johns Ter. TR18 38 E3
St Marys St. TR18 38 E3
St Marys Ter. TR18 38 E4
St Michaels St. TR18 38 E3
St Michaels Ter. TR18 38 D3
St Peters Hill. TR18 39 C7
St Peters Pl. TR18 39 C7
St Phillip St. TR18 38 E3
*St Warren St, Barwis Hill. TR18 38 E3
School La. TR18 38 F1
Sona Merg. TR18 38 C2
South Pl. TR18 38 D4
Stanford Ter. TR18 38 D4
Station Rd. TR18 38 E3
Strand. TR18 39 C7
Taroveor Rd. TR18 38 D3
Taroveor Ter. TR18 38 E4
Tencreek Av. TR18 38 D4
The Close. TR18 38 D2
The Coombe. TR18 39 A6
The Esplanade. TR18 39 D5
The Fradgan. TR18 39 C7
The Green. TR18 39 C7
The Mead Houses. TR18 38 F1
The Place. TR18 38 F3
The Quay. TR18 38 E4
The Square. TR18 38 F3
The Terrace. TR18 38 E4
Thornberry Ter. TR18 38 E3
Toltuff Cres. TR18 39 C5
Toltuff Rd. TR18 39 C5
Tolver Pl. TR18 38 D3
Tolver Rd. TR18 38 D3
Treassowe Rd. TR18 38 E3
Treban Rd. TR18 39 B5
Tredarvah Dri. TR18 38 C4
Tredarvah Rd. TR18 38 C4
Tredavoe La. TR18 39 B7
Tregarth Pl. TR18 39 B5
Tregie. TR18 39 A6
Treglyn Clo. TR18 39 B7
*Tregoddick Clo, Vingoes La. TR20 38 A1
Tremaine Clo. TR18 38 B3
Tremenheere Rd. TR18 38 D3
Treneere La. TR18 38 C2
Treneere Rd. TR18 38 D3
Treneglos Ter. TR18 39 C6
Trenoweth Cres. TR18 39 B5
Trenoweth Rd. TR18 39 B5
Trerew Rd. TR18 39 B5
Tretorvic Ter. TR18 38 B2
Trevale. TR18 38 C4
Trevarrack Pl. TR18 38 F2
Trevarrack Rd. TR18 38 E1
Trevean Rd. TR18 38 D4
Trevena Clo. TR18 39 C5
Trevena Rd. TR18 39 C5
Treveneth Cres. TR18 39 B8
Trewartha Ter. TR18 38 E3
Trewarvas Rd. TR18 39 C8
Trewarveneth St. TR18 39 C7
Treweath Rd. TR18 38 D2
Trewithen Rd. TR18 38 D4
Trezela Rd. TR18 38 D4
Trythogga Rd. TR18 38 F2
Under Chapel. TR18 39 E5
Union St. TR18 38 E4
Vellan Hoggan. TR18 38 F2
Victoria Pl. TR18 38 D4
Victoria Sq. TR18 38 E4
Vingoes La. TR18 38 A1
Voundervour La. TR18 38 E4
Weeths Cotts. TR18 38 D4
Wellfields. TR18 38 D4
Wellington Ter. TR18 38 D4
Wesley St. TR18 38 C2
West Ter. TR18 39 C6
Wharf Rd. TR18 38 E4
Wharfside. TR18 38 E4
*Wherry Town, The Esplanade. TR18 39 D5
Windsor Ter. TR18 38 D3
Wood St. TR18 38 E4
York St. TR18 38 D3

PERRANPORTH

Beach La. TR6 41 C2
Beach Rd. TR6 41 C2
Bolenna La. TR6 41 B5
Bolingey Rd. TR6 41 D6
Boscawen Gdns. TR6 41 B3
Boscawen Rd. TR6 41 C4
Cliff Rd. TR6 41 B2
Coombe View. TR6 41 A5
Droskyn Clo. TR6 41 A3
Droskyn Point. TR6 41 A2
Droskyn Way. TR6 41 A3
Eureka Vale. TR6 41 D2
Fuller Rd. TR6 41 A4
Grannys La. TR6 41 C5
Halveor Ct. TR6 41 D2
Hanover Clo. TR6 41 B3
Hental. TR6 41 C4
Higher Bolenna. TR6 41 A4
Joseph's Court. TR6 41 D1
Lamore Clo. TR6 41 D4
Liskey Hill. TR6 41 C3
Liskey Hill Cres. TR6 41 C4
Lower Hillcrest. TR6 41 B4
Lower Tywarhayle. TR6 41 B3
Miners Ct. TR6 41 B3
Pensilva. TR6 41 C5
Percy Davey Clo. TR6 41 D1
Perran Coombe. TR6 41 A6
Ponsmere Rd. TR6 41 D2
Ridgeway. TR6 41 D3
St Georges Hill. TR6 41 A4
St Michaels Rd. TR6 41 C4
St Pirans Rd. TR6 41 C2
Sandy Bay Holiday Flats. TR6 41 D1
Somerville Rd. TR6 41 C5
Station Rd. TR6 41 D2
Sunnyside. TR6 41 D4
The Gounce. TR6 41 C2
The Promenade. TR6 41 C2
Tredinnick Way. TR6 41 A4
Tregonning Ct. TR6 41 D2
Tregundy Ct. TR6 41 B2
Tregundy Rd. TR6 41 A4
Trevalga Clo. TR6 41 C4
Trevian Clo. TR6 41 C4
Tywarnhayle Rd. TR6 41 B3
Upper Hillcrest. TR6 41 B4
Wainsway. TR6 41 C3
Welway. TR6 41 D5
Wheal Leisure. TR6 41 C3
Wheal Leisure Clo. TR6 41 C3

REDRUTH

Adelaide Rd. TR15 43 F4
Agar Cres. TR15 42 A5
Agar Rd. TR15 42 A5
Agar Way. TR15 42 A5
Albany Ct. TR15 43 G6
Albany Gdns. TR15 43 G5
Albany Rd. TR15 43 F4
Alma Pl. TR15 43 F4
Ambrose Ct. TR15 43 H1
Appin Gdns. TR15 42 A4
Back Lane West. TR15 43 E4
Balkin Way. TR15 42 A4
Balmoral Ter. TR15 43 E3
Barncoose La. TR15 42 B5
Barncoose Ter. TR15 42 C4
Bassett Rd, Treleigh. TR16 43 E1
Bassett Rd, Paynter's Lane End. TR16 42 A1
Basset St. TR15 43 F4
Beacon View Pk. TR16 42 B1
Beauchamps Mdw. TR15 43 G6
Beckett Clo. TR15 43 G4
Bellevue. TR15 43 F3
Blights Row. TR15 43 E3
Blowinghouse Hill. TR15 42 D4
Bond St. TR15 43 F4
Boscarn Rd. TR15 43 G3
Boscoppa Clo. TR15 43 G1
Bosmeor Park. TR15 42 A4
Bosvean Gdns. TR16 42 A2
Broad La. TR15 42 A3
Bucketts Hill. TR15 43 F6
Bullers Ter. TR15 43 G3
Cal Hill. TR15 43 G5
Camborne Scorrier By-Pass. TR15 42 A3
Carbis Ct. TR15 43 E3
Cardrew Clo. TR15 43 E2
Cardrew Ter. TR15 43 G3
Cardrew Way. TR15 43 F2
Carn Brea Village. TR15 42 D5
Castle View Clo. TR15 43 E2
Channel View Ter. TR15 43 F4
Chapel St. TR15 43 E4
Chapel Ter. TR15 42 B4
Chariot Rd. TR15 42 B4
Chili Rd. TR15 42 B4
Church La. TR15 42 D5
Chynoon Gdns. TR15 42 A4
Claremont Rd. TR15 43 E3
Clarence Villas. TR15 43 G2
Clifton Rd. TR15 42 A3
Clijah Clo. TR15 43 G6
Clijah La. TR15 43 G6
Clijah Ter. TR15 43 F6
Clinton Clo. TR15 43 F5
Clinton Pass. TR15 43 F4
Clinton Rd. TR15 43 F4
Close Hill. TR15 43 E2
Coach La. TR15 43 E5
Colebrook Clo. TR15 43 E3
College La. TR15 43 H1
Coronation Rd. TR15 43 G5
Crembling Well. TR15 42 B4
Cross St. TR15 43 E4
Dopps Ter. TR15 43 F3
Dreysen Clo. TR15 42 A2
Druids Rd. TR15 42 B5
Drump Rd. TR15 43 F3
East End. TR15 43 F3
East Park. TR15 43 G3
East Pool Park. TR15 42 A4
Edmund Rd. TR15 43 E2
Elm Clo. TR15 42 B5
Euny Clo. TR15 42 D5
Falmouth Rd. TR15 43 E4
Fords Row. TR15 43 F4
Fore St. TR15 43 F4
Forth an Praze. TR15 42 A3
Forth an Ryn. TR15 43 G5
Forth Noweth. TR15 43 E4
Forth Scol. TR15 42 A4
Forthveor. TR15 43 H1
Foundry Row. TR15 43 E3
Garby La. TR15 43 G6
Gas La. TR15 43 F4
Gilly Fields. TR15 43 E5
Gilly Hill. TR15 43 F5
Gladstone Ter. TR15 43 F3
Glen Leigh. TR15 43 E2
Glendale Cres. TR15 43 G5
Graham Rd. TR15 43 G4
Green La. TR15 43 E3
Green Lane Vean. TR15 43 E3
Grenifer Rd. TR15 42 A3
Gweal-an-Top. TR15 43 G3
Harmony Clo. TR15 43 E2
Harrison Gdns. TR15 42 A4
Hawthorn Clo. TR15 43 F2
Heanton Ter. TR15 43 F4
Henvor Clo. TR15 43 G2
Highburrow La. TR15 42 A5
Higher Broad La. TR15 42 A3
Higher Fore St. TR15 43 F4
Higher Mount Ambrose La. TR15 43 G2
Higher North Country. TR16 43 E1
Higher West Tolgus. TR15 42 A3
Highland Park. TR15 43 G4
Highway La. TR15 43 G2
Hoskings Row. TR15 43 E4
Ilogan Park. TR16 42 A2
INDUSTRIAL & RETAIL:
Barncoose Ind Est. TR15 42 B5
Pool Ind Est. TR15 42 A5
Treleigh Ind Est. TR15 43 F1
West Cornwall Enterprise Centre Business Link. TR15 43 G2
Jenkins Ter. TR15 43 F3
Johns Pk. TR15 43 E3
Jon Davey Dri. TR15 43 F1
Kestrel Way. TR16 42 A2
Killiers Ct. TR15 42 A4
Killiers Field. TR15 42 A4
King St. TR15 43 E3
Knights Way. TR15 43 G2
Lamanva Rd. TR16 42 A1
Little Gilly Hill. TR15 43 F5
Little Vauxhall. TR15 43 E3
Lower Barncoose. TR15 42 C4
Lower Broad La. TR15 42 A2
Lower Cardrew La. TR15 43 F3
Manor Gdns. TR15 43 E3
Martinvale Av. TR15 43 H1
Mennaye Gdns. TR15 42 A4
Merritts Hill. TR16 42 A2
Miners Row. TR15 43 F3
Montague Av. TR15 43 E3
Moorfield Rd. TR15 42 A4
Morla La. TR15 43 E2
Mount Ambrose. TR15 43 G2
Mount Carbis Gdns. TR15 43 G5
Mount Carbis Rd. TR15 43 G5
Murdoch Clo. TR15 43 E2
Nettells Hill. TR15 43 E3
New Cut. TR15 43 E3
New La. TR15 43 H1
New Portreath Rd. TR16 42 D1
North Pool Clo. TR15 42 A3
North Pool Rd. TR15 42 A3
North St. TR15 43 E3
Old Portreath Rd. TR15 42 C1
Park Rd. TR15 43 F5
Park Leven. TR16 42 A2
Paynters La. TR16 42 A1
Pencarrow Rd. TR16 42 A1
Penders La. TR15 43 E3
Pengover Parc. TR15 43 F2
Penhalle Estate. TR15 43 F2
Penlean Clo. TR15 43 G1
Penpont Rd. TR15 43 G2
Penryn St. TR15 43 E4
Penwartha Rd. TR16 42 A1
Penwartha Vean. TR16 42 A1
Plain An Gwarry. TR15 43 E3
Polbathic Rd. TR15 43 G3
Poldark Rd. TR16 42 A1
Poldue Clo. TR15 43 G2
Polgooth Clo. TR15 43 G2
Polruan Rd. TR15 43 G3
Pond La. TR15 43 E3
Railway Villas. TR15 42 C5
Raymond Rd. TR15 43 F4
Redruth By-Pass. TR15 42 D4
Redruth Coombe. TR15 42 D6
Redruth Highway. TR15 43 H1
Redvers Heights. TR15 43 F5
Richards La. TR16 42 A2
River Row. TR15 42 C4
Roachs Row. TR15 43 E3
Roekindale Clo. TR15 42 B4
Rose Hill. TR15 43 E3
Rose Row. TR15 43 E3
Roseland Gdns. TR15 43 F3
St Day Rd. TR15 43 G4
St Uny Cres. TR15 42 D5
Sandy La. TR15 43 G3
School La. TR15 43 G3
Sea View Ter. TR15 43 F4
Shoot Row. TR15 43 F4
South Albany Rd. TR15 43 F5
South Downs. TR15 43 G6
South Park. TR15 42 D4
South Park Clo. TR15 42 D5
Southgate St. TR15 43 F5
Spar La. TR15 42 A2
Sparnon Clo. TR15 43 F5
Sparnon Hill. TR15 43 F5
Sparnon Ter. TR15 43 F5
Stamps La. TR15 42 B4
Stanley Way. TR15 43 F2
Station Hill. TR15 43 F4
Station Rd. TR15 43 F4
Strawberry Clo. TR15 43 F2
Strawberry La. TR15 43 E2
Sunny Side. TR15 43 F4
Sunnyside Parc. TR15 42 A2
Sycamore Dri. TR15 42 A3
Symons Ter. TR15 43 E4
Talgos Clo. TR15 41 H1
Talveneth. TR15 43 F3
Tangye Rd. TR15 42 A4
Tarewaste. TR15 42 C4
The Paddock. TR15 43 G6
Tolgus Hill. TR15 42 D3
Tolgus Mount. TR15 42 C2
Tolgus Pl. TR15 42 D3
Tolgus Vean. TR15 42 D3
Tolgus Wartha. TR15 43 E3
Town Farm. TR15 43 F5

Trebarva Clo. TR15 42 D3
Treforthlan. TR16 42 A1
Trefusis Rd. TR15 43 F4
Trefusis Ter. TR15 43 F4
Treganoon Rd. TR15 43 G1
*Tregullan, Sunnyside
Parc. TR16 42 A2
Trelawney Av. TR15 43 H1
Treleigh Av. TR15 43 E3
Treleigh Ter. TR15 43 E3
Treliske Rd. TR15 43 G2
Treloweth Rd. TR15 42 A4
Treloweth Way. TR15 42 A4
Tremore Rd. TR15 43 G3
Trenear Clo. TR15 43 G2
Treruffe Hill. TR15 43 F4
Treruffe Ter. TR15 43 F4
Tresadens Rd. TR15 43 H1
Treskerby. TR15 43 H1
Trevanion Ter. TR15 42 D5
Trevelthan Rd. TR16 42 A1
Trevener Mews. TR15 43 E3
Trevingey Clo. TR15 42 D5
Trevingey Parc. TR15 42 D5
Trevingey Cres. TR15 42 D5
Trevingey Rd. TR15 42 D5
Trevithick Rd. TR15 42 A5
Trewans Ter. TR15 43 E2
Trewirgie Hill. TR15 43 E5
Trewirgie Rd. TR15 43 E5
Trewirgie Vean. TR15 43 E5
Valley Gdns. TR16 42 B1
Vista-del-Mar. TR15 43 G3
Vorfield Clo. TR15 43 E2
Wesley St. TR15 43 F4
West End. TR15 43 E4
West Park. TR15 42 D4
West Tolgus. TR15 42 B2
West Trevingey. TR15 42 D5
West Trewirgie Rd.
TR15 43 E5
Westbourne Heights.
TR15 43 E5
Wheal Agar. TR 42 A4
Wheal Fortune La.
TR15 42 B5
Wheal Tehidy La. TR15 42 C4
Wheal Trefusis. TR15 43 G6
Wilson Way. TR15 42 A5

ST. AGNES

Angwin Av. TR5 44 B5
Beaconsfield Pl. TR5 44 B5
Bolster Clo. TR5 44 B6
Brecon Clo. TR5 44 B3
British Rd. TR5 44 C5
Castle Meadows. TR5 44 C5
Chegwyn Gdns. TR5 44 B4
Churchtown. TR5 44 B4
Durning Rd. TR5 44 A6
Goonown La. TR5 44 C6
Goonown Rd. TR5 44 C6
Goonvrea Rd. TR5 44 B6
Grenville Dri. TR5 44 D4
Kemps Clo. TR5 44 B5
Kerensa Gdns. TR5 44 C6
Lambourne Dri. TR5 44 B6
Lawrence Rd. TR5 44 B6
Middlegates. TR5 44 B6
Pengarth. TR5 44 B5
Penwinnick Av. TR5 44 B6
Penwinnick Parc. TR5 44 B6
Penwinnick Rd. TR5 44 B6
Polbreen Av. TR5 44 B5
Polbreen La. TR5 44 B6
Quay Rd. TR5 44 C2
Rocky La. TR5 44 B3
Rosemundy. TR5 44 B4
Stippy Stappy. TR5 44 B4
Town Hill. TR5 44 B4
Tregrease Rd. TR5 44 A4
Trelawney Rd. TR5 44 B5
Trevaunance Clo. TR5 44 A3
Trevaunance Rd. TR5 44 A3
Trevose Clo. TR5 44 A4
Vicarage Rd. TR5 44 B5
Water La. TR5 44 C5
Wheal Friendly La. TR5 44 B3
Wheal Kitty. TR5 44 A4
Wheal Kitty La. TR5 44 C4
Wheal Quoit Av. TR5 44 A4
Whites Clo. TR5 44 B5

Whitworth Clo. TR5 44 A6

ST. AUSTELL

Agar Rd. PL25 47 F2
Albert Rd. PL25 46 D5
Alexandra Rd. PL25 47 E5
Arena Cres. PL25 47 H3
Avon Clo. PL25 47 H3
Aylmer Sq. PL25 46 C5
Bay View Park. PL25 47 F2
Beacon Clo. PL25 47 H2
Beech La. PL25 46 D5
Beech Rd. PL25 46 D5
Belmont Rd. PL25 46 D6
Bethel Rd. PL25 47 G3
Biddicks Ct. PL25 46 C4
Blowing House Hill.
PL25 46 B4
Blowing House La.
PL25 46 B4
Boconnoc Rd. PL25 46 D6
Bodmin Rd. PL25 46 C4
Boldventure Av. PL25 47 H3
Boldventure Clo. PL25 47 H3
Boldventure Rd. PL25 47 H3
Boscarne Cres. PL25 47 G5
Boscoppa Rd. PL25 47 G3
Bossiney Rd. PL25 46 D6
Bownder Vean. PL25 47 G3
Bramley Clo. PL25 47 F4
Bridge Ct. PL25 47 G4
Bridge Rd. PL25 46 B5
Brockstone Rd. PL25 47 H2
Brookside. PL25 47 F3
Bucklers La. PL25 47 H3
Cannis Rd. PL25 47 E1
Carclaze Rd. PL25 47 F1
Carlyon Rd. PL25 46 D4
Carnsmerry Cres. PL25 47 E4
Carrickowel Cres. PL25 47 H2
Central Av. PL25 47 F3
Century Clo. PL25 47 F1
Chapel Field. PL25 47 H3
Charles Clo. PL25 47 G5
Charlestown Rd. PL25 47 G5
Cherry Tree Mews.
PL25 46 D5
Chippodds Clo. PL25 46 A5
Chisholme Clo. PL25 46 D5
Chough Cres. PL25 47 G4
Church Rd. PL25 47 H5
Church St. PL25 46 C5
Clarence Rd. PL25 46 B4
Clayborne Clo. PL25 47 F1
Clifden Rd. PL25 46 B5
Clinton Dri. PL25 46 B5
Coach House La. PL25 46 C4
Colenso Pl. PL25 46 D5
College Grn. PL25 46 C5
Cormorant Dri. PL25 47 G4
Court Gdns. PL25 46 C5
Courtland Cres. PL25 47 H3
Courtney Rd. PL25 47 F3
Cromwell Rd. PL25 47 F5
Cross La. PL25 46 D5
Daniel Clo. PL25 47 H3
Daniels La. PL25 47 H3
Dennison Av. PL25 47 H3
Dithmarschen Way.
PL25 46 C6
Dobell Rd. PL25 47 F4
Doulton Rd. PL25 47 H4
Duke St. PL25 46 C5
East Hill. PL25 46 D5
Eastbourne Clo. PL25 47 E6
Eastbourne Rd. PL25 46 D5
Eastfield Way. PL25 47 G3
Eddystone Rd. PL25 47 F2
Edgecumbe Grn. PL25 46 A4
Edgecumbe Rd. PL25 46 A4
Eliot Rd. PL25 47 F4
Elizabeth Rd. PL25 47 G1
Emlyn Field. PL25 47 G1
Eton Rd. PL25 47 E5
Fairbourne Rd. PL25 47 F4
Fairfield Clo. PL25 47 H5
Fore St. PL25 46 C5
Franklyn Clo. PL25 47 H3
Gannet Dri. PL25 47 G4
Gerrans Clo. PL25 47 H3
Glen Dale Clo. PL25 47 H3
Glen Dale Cres. PL25 47 H3

Glenview. PL25 46 B5
Globe Yd. PL25 46 C4
Gover Rd. PL25 46 A3
Graham Av. PL25 47 E4
Grants Walk. PL25 46 C4
Greensplat Rd. PL25 46 A1
Gribben Clo. PL25 47 E1
Gribben Rd. PL25 47 E1
Grosvenor Pl. PL25 46 B4
Grove Rd. PL25 46 B4
Gwallon Rd. PL25 47 F2
Gwel-An-Mor. PL25 47 G2
Hallane Rd. PL25 47 G1
Hawthorn Clo. PL25 47 G2
Hazel Clo. PL25 47 G2
High Cross St. PL25 46 C4
Higher Tremena. PL25 46 C3
Higher Woodside.
PL25 46 A4
Highfield Av. PL25 47 E5
Hill Park Cres. PL25 46 A6
Hillside. PL25 47 H5
Hillside Rd. PL25 47 E3
Holmbush Rd. PL25 47 G5
Horsley Rise. PL25 46 D5
Jeryon Clo. PL25 47 F1
Keryor Cres. PL25 47 H2
Killyvarder Way. PL25 47 H2
Kingfisher Dri. PL25 47 G4
Kings Av. PL25 46 D5
Landrew Rd. PL25 47 G2
Larcombe Rd. PL25 47 G1
Laura Dri. PL25 47 H2
Ledrah Gdns. PL25 46 B5
Ledrah Rd. PL25 46 B5
Lewis Way. PL25 47 E2
Long Park Way. PL25 47 E2
Lookout La. PL25 47 E2
Lostwood Rd. PL25 47 E3
Lower Sawles Rd.
PL25 46 D6
Lower Woodside. PL25 46 A4
Lyndhurst Av. PL25 47 G4
Lyons Rd. PL25 47 H4
Lytton Pl. PL25 47 F4
Manor Clo. PL25 47 F3
Margaret Av. PL25 47 F4
Market Hill. PL25 46 C4
Market St. PL25 46 C5
Mayfield Clo. PL25 47 H4
Meadow Clo. PL25 47 G1
Meadway. PL25 47 F3
Menabilly Rd. PL25 47 E2
Menacuddle Hill. PL25 46 C4
Menacuddle La. PL25 46 C3
Meneage Villas. PL25 46 B5
Menear Rd. PL25 47 G3
Minton Clo. PL25 47 H4
Mitchell Rd. PL25 47 G4
Moorland Rd. PL25 46 C5
Morcom Clo. PL25 47 G2
Morleigh Clo. PL25 47 F5
Morven Rd. PL25 46 A4
Mount Charles Rd.
PL25 47 G5
Mount Stamper Rd.
PL25 46 D2
Mountstephen Clo.
PL25 46 A5
North East
Distribution Rd. PL25 47 G1
North Hill Park. PL25 46 D4
North St. PL25 46 C4
Old Lawn School La.
PL25 46 B5
Old Vicarage Pl. PL25 46 C5
Orchard Clo. PL25 47 F4
Orchard Gro. PL25 46 B4
Palace Rd. PL25 46 D4
Park Rd. PL25 46 C5
Park Way. PL25 47 F3
Penhaligon Way. PL25 47 G3
Penmere Rd. PL25 47 G4
Pennor Rd. PL25 46 D5
Penrice Parc. PL25 47 H5
Pensylva. PL25 47 E6
Pentewan Rd. PL25 46 C6
Penwinnick Rd. PL25 46 B6
Phernyssick Rd. PL25 47 F1
Polkyth Rd. PL25 47 F4
Polmarth Clo. PL25 47 F1
Polmear Rd. PL25 47 G5
Poltair Av. PL25 47 E3
Poltair Cres. PL25 47 E3
Poltair Rd. PL25 47 E4
Pondhu Cres. PL25 46 B5

Pondhu Rd. PL25 46 C5
Porthpean Rd. PL25 47 G5
Pridmouth Rd. PL25 47 E2
Prince Charles Pk.
PL25 47 E3
Prince Charles Rd.
PL25 47 E3
Priory Rd. PL25 46 C4
Queens Rd. PL25 47 E5
Ranelagh Rd. PL25 47 F4
Rashleigh Mews. PL25 47 H5
Rashleigh Pl. PL25 47 F4
River Walk. PL25 46 B5
Robartes Pl. PL25 47 E3
Robert Eliot Ct. PL25 47 B5
Ropehaven Clo. PL25 47 E1
Ropehaven Rd. PL25 47 E2
Roslyn Clo. PL25 47 G2
St Pirans Clo. PL25 47 F1
Sandy Hill. PL25 47 F5
Sawles Rd. PL25 46 D5
Sharaman Clo. PL25 47 G3
Shelley Rd. PL25 47 H4
Slades Rd. PL25 47 F2
South St. PL25 46 C5
Southbourne Rd. PL25 47 E6
Sparnon Clo. PL25 46 B4
Springfield Clo. PL25 47 G3
Stennack Rd. PL25 47 G3
Stoney La. PL25 46 C4
Sycamore Av. PL25 47 E2
Sydney Clo. PL25 46 C5
Sylvan Clo. PL25 47 H2
Symons Clo. PL25 47 H2
Tewington Pl. PL25 46 B4
The Copse. PL25 47 G3
The Oaks. PL25 47 B5
The Sycamores. PL25 46 D4
Thornpark Rd. PL25 47 H3
Timber Clo. PL25 46 B4
Tolcarne Clo. PL25 47 F6
Tregarne Ter. PL25 46 D4
Tregonissey Clo. PL25 47 E3
Tregonissey Rd. PL25 47 E3
Trelake Rd. PL25 46 B4
Trelawney Rd. PL25 47 F4
Tremayne Rd. PL25 47 F4
Trembear Rd. PL25 46 A3
Tremena Gdns. PL25 46 C3
Tremena Rd. PL25 46 C4
Trenance Hill. PL25 46 A3
Trenance Pl. PL25 46 B4
Trenance Rd. PL25 46 A3
Trenarren View. PL25 47 G1
Trenowah Rd. PL25 47 H3
Trevanion Rd. PL25 46 B4
Trevarrick Rd. PL25 46 B4
Trevarthian Rd. PL25 46 B4
Trevear Clo. PL25 47 E6
Treverbyn Gdns. PL25 47 G3
Treverbyn Rd. PL25 47 E1
Trevithick Rd. PL25 47 E5
Trevone Cres. PL25 46 A4
Trewhiddle Rd. PL25 46 C6
Trinity St. PL25 46 C5
Truro Rd. PL25 46 A6
Turnavean Rd. PL25 46 A3
Victoria Rd. PL25 47 F5
Watering Hill Clo. PL25 47 F5
Watersedge Rd. PL25 46 B4
Wedgwood Rd. PL25 47 H4
Wesley Pl. PL25 47 F5
West Hill. PL25 46 C5
Westbourne Dri. PL25 46 B5
Whieldon Rd. PL25 47 H4
Woodland Clo. PL25 47 H5
Woodland Rd. PL25 47 H4
Worcester Rd. PL25 47 H4

ST. BLAZEY/PAR

Aberdeen Clo . PL24 48 D1
Anjardyn Pl. PL24 49 F3
Ash Clo. PL24 48 B5
Ash Gro. PL24 48 B5
Belmont St. PL24 49 G2
Biscovey Rd. PL24 48 A5
Bobs Rd. PL24 48 B4
Bodelva Rd. PL24 48 A2
Chapel Rd. PL24 49 E4
Chapel Ter. PL24 48 C1
Church St,
St Blazey. PL24 48 C2

Church St,
Tywardreath. PL24 49 G2
Chyandor Clo. PL24 48 D4
Cornhill Rd. PL24 48 A2
Cypress Av. PL25 48 A6
Doubletrees. PL24 48 B4
Driving La. PL24 49 E1
Duke St. PL24 48 C1
Eastcliffe Rd. PL24 49 F4
Eden Clo. PL24 48 C5
Edgecumbe Ter. PL24 48 B4
Elderfield Clo. PL24 49 G2
Fore St,
St Blazey. PL24 48 C1
Fore St,
Tywardreath. PL24 49 G2
Glen View. PL24 49 G2
Grove Rd. PL24 48 B4
Harbour Rd. PL24 49 E5
Helleur Clo. PL24 48 D4
Hillside Av. PL24 48 B5
Kilhallon Woodlands.
PL24 49 E1
Lamb Park. PL24 48 D4
Lamellyn Rd. PL24 48 C4
Landreath Pl. PL24 49 H2
Legion La. PL24 49 H2
Lesnewth. PL24 48 A2
Luxulyan Rd. PL24 48 A2
Manor Vw. PL24 48 B5
Meadow Dri. PL24 48 B5
Middleway. PL24 49 E4
Moorland Rd. PL24 49 E4
Mount Bennett Rd.
PL24 49 H2
Mount Cres. PL24 49 E5
Mount Rd. PL24 49 E5
Mount Ter. PL24 48 C4
North St. PL24 49 G2
Old Roselyon Cres.
PL24 48 D3
Old Roselyon Rd. PL24 48 D4
Par Grn. PL24 49 E4
Par La. PL24 48 C4
Par Moor Rd. PL24 48 A6
Pembroke Clo. PL24 49 E5
Penarwyn Rd. PL24 48 C4
Penarwyn Woods.
PL24 48 C4
Pennys La. PL24 48 A5
Penstrasse Pl. PL24 49 H1
Poldark Gdns. PL24 48 B4
Poldrea. PL24 49 H2
Polgover Way. PL24 48 C4
Polgrean Pl. PL24 48 D2
Polmear Parc. PL24 49 G4
Polmear Rd. PL24 49 F4
Polpey La. PL24 49 H4
Priory Clo. PL24 49 F3
Quarry Ter. PL24 48 D1
Rebecca Clo. PL24 48 D1
Rose Hill Rd. PL24 48 B4
Roselyon Pl. PL24 48 D3
St Andrews Rd. PL24 49 E1
St Andrews Ter. PL24 49 E2
St Annes Rd. PL24 48 B5
St Austell Rd. PL24 48 A5
St Benedicts Clo. PL24 49 G3
St Blazey Rd. PL24 48 D3
St Marys Rd. PL24 48 C4
St Sampsons Clo. PL24 49 H2
School Clo. PL24 48 B5
Sea View Ter. PL24 48 C1
Southpark Rd. PL24 49 F3
Southview Rd. PL24 48 B5
Station Rd. PL24 48 D2
Swallowfield Clo. PL24 49 G2
Tehidy Rd. PL24 49 F3
The Lawn. PL24 48 D1
The Mews. PL24 48 D1
Tredenham Clo. PL24 49 E4
Treffry Way. PL24 48 B5
Trenant Rd. PL24 49 H3
Trenovissick Rd. PL24 48 A5
Trenython Rd. PL24 48 C5
Teryn Clo. PL24 48 C3
Trevance Pk. PL24 49 G2
Trevarweneth Rd. PL24 48 B4
Tywardreath Hill. PL24 49 G4
Vernon Villas. PL24 48 B4
Vicarage Rd. PL24 49 F3
Vine Pl. PL24 49 G2
Well St. PL24 49 G3
Wood La. PL24 49 G2
Woodland Av. PL24 49 F2

ST. COLUMB MAJOR

Bank St. TR9 — 45 C2
Barn La. TR9 — 45 B4
Bospolvans Rd. TR9 — 45 A3
Bosworgey Clo. TR9 — 45 A3
Bridge. TR9 — 45 C1
Bridge Hill. TR9 — 45 C1
Broad St. TR9 — 45 C2
Carloggas Gro. TR9 — 45 A4
Carloggas Way. TR9 — 45 A3
Dinas. TR9 — 45 A3
East St. TR9 — 45 C2
Fair St. TR9 — 45 B3
Fore St. TR9 — 45 C3
Glebe Clo. TR9 — 45 B2
Gordon Pl. TR9 — 45 C2
Halveor Clo. TR9 — 45 A3
Halveor La. TR9 — 45 A2
Hawkens Way. TR9 — 45 A4
Lawthorn Clo. TR9 — 45 A4
High Cross. TR9 — 45 A4
Higher East St. TR9 — 45 C3
Highfield Av. TR9 — 45 C3
Hill Crest Clo. PL25 — 45 C3
INDUSTRIAL & RETAIL:
St Columb Ind Est. TR9 — 45 A4
Maple Clo. TR9 — 45 A4
Market Pl. TR9 — 45 C2
Meadow Rise. TR9 — 45 C2
New Rd. TR9 — 45 C1
Newquay Rd. TR9 — 45 B3
Old Rectory Dri. TR9 — 45 C1
Old Rectory Mews. TR9 — 45 B1
Parsons Garth. TR9 — 45 D1
Penkernick Way. TR9 — 45 A4
Praze an Croner. TR9 — 45 B4
Rachels Way. TR9 — 45 C4
Rosewin Mews. TR9 — 45 C2
Ruskin Ct. TR9 — 45 B5
South Pk. TR9 — 45 B4
Springfield Pl. TR9 — 45 B4
Station Rd. TR9 — 45 B3
Trekenning Rd. TR9 — 45 B3
Trelawney Parc. TR9 — 45 B4
Trethewey Clo. TR9 — 45 B4
Treventon Rise. TR9 — 45 C3
Union Hill. TR9 — 45 C2
Union Sq. TR9 — 45 C2
Victoria St. TR9 — 45 B2
West Park. TR9 — 45 B3
West St. TR9 — 45 C3
Wreford Clo. TR9 — 45 A4

ST. IVES

Academy Pl. TR26 — 51 J8
Academy Ter. TR26 — 51 J8
Alan Harvey Clo. TR26 — 50 B6
Albany Ter. TR26 — 50 D3
Albert Rd. TR26 — 50 C3
Alexandra Pl. TR26 — 50 A4
Alexandra Rd. TR26 — 50 A4
Alexandra Row. TR26 — 50 A4
Alexandra Ter. TR26 — 50 A4
Atlantic Ter. TR26 — 51 J8
Ayr La. TR26 — 51 J8
Ayr Ter. TR26 — 50 B3
Back Rd East. TR26 — 51 K7
Back Rd West. TR26 — 51 J7
Back St. TR26 — 51 J8
Bahavella Dri. TR26 — 50 C4
Baileys La. TR26 — 51 J7
Barnawoon. TR26 — 51 J8
Barnoon Hill. TR26 — 51 J8
Barrepta Clo. TR26 — 51 H5
Beach Rd. TR26 — 51 A3
Bedford Pl TR26 — 51 J8
Bedford Rd. TR26 — 51 J8
Belliair Ter. TR26 — 51 J8
Belyars Clo. TR26 — 50 D4
Belyars La. TR26 — 50 C4
Bethesda Hill. TR26 — 51 K7
Bethesda Pl. TR26 — 51 K7
Bishops Rd. TR26 — 50 C3
Boskerris Cres. TR26 — 51 G5

Boskerris Rd. TR26 — 51 G5
Bowling Green Ter. TR26 — 51 J8
Bullans La. TR26 — 50 B3
Bullans Ter. TR26 — 50 B3
Bunkers Hill. TR26 — 51 J7
Burrow Rd. TR26 — 51 J7
Burthallan La. TR26 — 50 A4
Camaret Dri. TR26 — 50 C4
Carbis Valley Rd. TR26 — 51 G5
Carn Ellis Rd. TR26 — 50 B4
Carncrows St. TR26 — 51 K7
Carnglaze Pl. TR26 — 51 K7
Carninney La. TR26 — 51 F6
Carnstabba Rd. TR26 — 50 B6
Carrack Dhu Ter. TR26 — 51 J8
Carthew Clo. TR26 — 50 A3
Carthew Ct. TR26 — 50 A3
Carthew Ter. TR26 — 50 A3
Carthew Way. TR26 — 50 A3
Channel Vw. TR26 — 50 B3
Chapel St. TR26 — 51 K8
Church Pl. TR26 — 51 J7
Chy An Dour Clo. TR26 — 50 A6
Clodgy Vw. TR26 — 51 J8
Corva Clo. TR26 — 50 B5
Corva Rd. TR26 — 50 B5
Count House La. TR26 — 51 F6
Court Cocking. TR26 — 51 J8
Crows An Eglos. TR26 — 50 A5
Dinas la Rd. TR26 — 50 C4
Dove St. TR26 — 50 C3
Enys Clo. TR26 — 51 G6
Fernlea Ter. TR26 — 51 K8
Fish St. TR26 — 51 J7
Fore St. TR26 — 51 J8
Fuggoe La. TR26 — 51 F5
Gabriel St. TR26 — 50 C3
Garth An Creet. TR26 — 50 B5
Gill An Creet. TR26 — 50 A5
Godrevy Ct. TR26 — 51 F5
Godrevy Ter. TR26 — 51 J8
Godrevy Ter, Carbis Bay. TR26 — 51 G6
Gwel An Wheal. TR26 — 50 B5
Gwel An Wheal Cres. TR26 — 50 B5
Gwelanmor Rd. TR26 — 51 G5
Hain Walk. TR26 — 51 E3
Headland Clo. TR26 — 51 H4
Headland Rd. TR26 — 51 H4
Hecla Dri. TR26 — 51 E5
Hellesvean. TR26 — 50 A5
Hellesvean Clo. TR26 — 50 A5
Hendra Vean. TR26 — 51 H5
Hendras Parc. TR26 — 51 H5
Hicks Ct. TR26 — 51 J7
High St. TR26 — 51 K8
Higher Boskerris. TR26 — 51 G6
Higher Stennack. TR26 — 50 A6
Higher Tregenna Rd. TR26 — 51 E5
Higher Trewidden Rd. TR26 — 50 C4
INDUSTRIAL & RETAIL:
Porthia Rd Ind Est. TR26 — 50 B6
Island Rd. TR26 — 51 J7
Island Sq. TR26 — 51 J7
Karenza Ct. TR26 — 51 H4
Kenidjack Clo. TR26 — 51 H5
Kew Vean. TR26 — 51 F5
Knill Clo. TR26 — 51 F6
Laity La. TR26 — 51 H6
Longstone Clo. TR26 — 51 H5
Manor Dri. TR26 — 51 E5
Market Pl. TR26 — 51 J8
Market Strand. TR26 — 51 K8
Menhir Clo. TR26 — 51 E6
Mount Zion. TR26 — 51 J7
Norway La. TR26 — 51 J7
Norway Sq. TR26 — 51 J7
Orange La. TR26 — 50 A3
Pannier La. TR26 — 51 F5
Parc An Creet. TR26 — 50 B5
Parc An Forth. TR26 — 50 B5
Parc An Stamps. TR26 — 50 A5
Parc Bean. TR26 — 50 B3
Parc Lowen. TR26 — 51 F6
Parc Owles. TR26 — 51 F5
Park En Gonwyn. TR26 — 51 H5
Pednolva Walk. TR26 — 51 K7
Pen An Gwel. TR26 — 50 B5
Pen Porth Av. TR26 — 50 A5

Penbeagle Clo. TR26 — 50 B5
Penbeagle Cres. TR26 — 50 B5
Penbeagle La. TR26 — 50 B5
Penbeagle Ter. TR26 — 50 B5
Penbeagle Way. TR26 — 50 B5
Penwith Clo. TR26 — 50 B5
Penwith Rd. TR26 — 50 B5
Poldhu Clo. TR26 — 51 H6
Polgarth Clo. TR26 — 51 H6
Polmennor Dri. TR26 — 51 G6
Polmeor Clo. TR26 — 51 G6
Polruan Clo. TR26 — 51 H6
Poltreen Clo. TR26 — 51 G6
Polwithen Dri. TR26 — 51 G6
Polwithen Gdns. TR26 — 51 F6
Pordenack Clo. TR26 — 51 H4
Porthia Clo. TR26 — 50 B5
Porthia Cres. TR26 — 50 B5
Porthia Rd. TR26 — 50 B6
Porthmeor. TR26 — 51 J8
Porthmeor Hill. TR26 — 51 J8
Porthmeor Rd. TR26 — 51 J7
Porthmeor Sq. TR26 — 51 J7
Porthrepta Rd. TR26 — 51 G4
Praze An Creet. TR26 — 50 A5
Primrose Valley. TR26 — 50 D3
Priors Clo. TR26 — 50 B6
Richmond Clo. TR26 — 51 G5
Richmond Pl. TR26 — 51 J8
Richmond Way. TR26 — 51 G5
Ros Lyn. TR26 — 51 F6
Rose La. TR26 — 51 J7
St Andrews St. TR26 — 51 K8
St Anta Rd. TR26 — 51 H5
St Eia St. TR26 — 51 K7
St Ives Rd. TR26 — 51 E5
St Johns Walk. TR26 — 50 A5
St Peters St. TR26 — 51 J7
Salubrious Ter. TR26 — 51 J8
Sandows La. TR26 — 50 B4
Sea View Pl. TR26 — 51 K7
Sea View Ter. TR26 — 50 C3
Sheilas Ct. TR26 — 51 H6
Skidden Hill. TR26 — 51 K8
Smeatons Pier. TR26 — 51 K7
Southfield Pl. TR26 — 50 B3
Spernan Clo. TR26 — 51 E5
Station Hill. TR26 — 51 K8
Steeple Clo. TR26 — 51 E5
Steeple La. TR26 — 51 E5
Steeple View Ct. TR26 — 51 G6
Stennack Gdns. TR26 — 50 B4
Street An Pol. TR26 — 51 K8
Street An Garrow. TR26 — 51 J8
Talland Rd. TR26 — 50 C3
Teetotal St. TR26 — 51 K7
The Burrows. TR26 — 50 B4
The Crescent. TR26 — 51 H6
The Digey. TR26 — 51 J7
The Meadow. TR26 — 51 J7
The Rope Walk. TR26 — 50 B4
The Stennack. TR26 — 50 C3
The Terrace. TR26 — 50 C3
The Warren. TR26 — 51 K8
The Wharf. TR26 — 51 J7
Tregarthen. TR26 — 50 B4
Tregenna Hill. TR26 — 51 K8
Tregenna Parc. TR26 — 51 E5
Tregenna Ter. TR26 — 51 K8
Tregos Rd. TR26 — 50 C3
Tregwary Rd. TR26 — 51 F5
Trelawney Av. TR26 — 50 B4
Trelawney Rd. TR26 — 50 B4
Treloyhan Clo. TR26 — 51 E5
Treloyhan Pk Rd. TR26 — 51 K4
Trelyon Av. TR26 — 50 C3
Tremar Rd. TR26 — 50 A4
Trencrom La. TR26 — 51 H6
Trenwith La. TR26 — 50 B5
Trenwith Pl. TR26 — 50 C3
Trerice Pl. TR26 — 50 B4
Trerice Rd. TR26 — 50 B4
Trevarrick Ct. TR26 — 51 F6
Treverbyn Rd. TR26 — 50 B4
Trewartha Clo. TR26 — 51 H6
Trewartha Est. TR26 — 51 H6
Trewidden Rd. TR26 — 50 C3
Valley Rd. TR26 — 51 F5
Venton Rd. TR26 — 51 E4
Victoria Pl. TR26 — 51 K7
Victoria Rd. TR26 — 51 J7
Virgin St. TR26 — 51 J7
Wesley Pl. TR26 — 50 B3
West Pier. TR26 — 51 K8

West Pl. TR26 — 51 J8
Westward Rd. TR26 — 50 B3
Wheal Dream. TR26 — 51 K7
Wheal Margery. TR26 — 51 G6
Wheal Speed Rd. TR26 — 51 F6
Wheal Venture Rd. TR26 — 51 E5
Wheal Whidden. TR26 — 51 F5
White House Clo. TR26 — 51 F6
Wills La. TR26 — 51 J8
Windsor Hill. TR26 — 50 B3

ST. JUST

Bank Sq. TR19 — 52 C3
Bethany Pl. TR19 — 52 C4
Bosorne Clo. TR19 — 52 A4
Bosorne Rd. TR19 — 52 A4
Bosorne St. TR19 — 52 B4
Bosorne Ter. TR19 — 52 A2
Boswedden Rd. TR19 — 52 A2
Cape Cornwall Rd. TR19 — 52 A3
Cape Cornwall St. TR19 — 52 B3
Carn Bosavern. TR19 — 52 C5
Carn Bosavern Clo. TR19 — 52 C5
Carrallack La. TR19 — 52 B5
Carrallack Mews. TR19 — 52 B5
Chapel Rd. TR19 — 52 B3
Chapel St. TR19 — 52 B3
Church St. TR19 — 52 C4
Fore St. TR19 — 52 C4
Lafrowda Clo. TR19 — 52 B4
Lafrowda Ter. TR19 — 52 C4
Market Sq. TR19 — 52 C3
Market St. TR19 — 52 B4
Nancherrow Hill. TR19 — 52 B2
Nancherrow Row. TR19 — 52 C1
Nancherrow Ter. TR19 — 52 C1
New Rd. TR19 — 52 D2
No Go By Hill. TR19 — 52 C1
North Row. TR19 — 52 C3
Old Foundry Clo. TR19 — 52 C3
Pednandrea. TR19 — 52 A2
Penzance Rd. TR19 — 52 A4
Pleasant Ter. TR19 — 52 A4
Princess St. TR19 — 52 A4
Queen St. TR19 — 52 A4
Regent Ter. TR19 — 52 A4
South Pl. TR19 — 52 B5
South Pl Gdns. TR19 — 52 B5
The Turnpike. TR19 — 52 D2
Tregeseal Row. TR19 — 52 D1
Tregeseal Ter. TR19 — 52 D1
Venton East Hill. TR19 — 52 D3
Venton East Sq. TR19 — 52 D3
Victoria Row. TR19 — 52 B4
Vounder Glaze. TR19 — 52 B4
West Pl. TR19 — 52 B4

SALTASH

Adit La. PL12 — 53 D2
Alamein Ct. PL12 — 53 C3
Alamein Rd. PL12 — 53 C3
Albert Rd. PL12 — 53 E3
Alexandra Sq. PL12 — 53 E3
Ashbirch Parc. PL12 — 53 A2
Babis Farm Clo. PL12 — 53 D3
Babis Farm Way. PL12 — 53 D3
Babis La. PL12 — 53 E4
Back Hill. PL12 — 53 B3
Barkers Hill. PL12 — 53 B3
Barn Park. PL12 — 53 B3
Barrow Down. PL12 — 53 A2
Beatrice Av. PL12 — 53 E1
Beaumont Ter. PL12 — 53 E1
Belle Vue Rd. PL12 — 53 C2
Beweys Park. PL12 — 53 B2
Birkdale Clo. PL12 — 53 B3
Biscombe Gdns. PL12 — 53 E2
*Boscundle Row, Fore St. PL12 — 53 E3
Briansway. PL12 — 53 C3
Broad Walk. PL12 — 53 C3
Brookdown Ter. PL12 — 53 D2

Brooking Way. PL12 — 53 B2
Brooks Hill. PL12 — 53 D1
Broom Hill. PL12 — 53 B3
Brunel Rd. PL12 — 53 B1
Buller Park. PL12 — 53 B2
Burnett Clo. PL12 — 53 B3
Burraton Rd. PL12 — 53 A1
Burry Park. PL12 — 53 B2
Butterdown. PL12 — 53 A2
Cabot Clo. PL12 — 53 D3
Callington Rd. PL12 — 53 B1
Caradan Ter. PL12 — 53 D2
Carew Gdns. PL12 — 53 B2
Carey Ct. PL12 — 53 C1
Carnoustie Dri. PL12 — 53 B3
Carrisbrooke Way. PL12 — 53 A2
Castle Ct. PL12 — 53 A3
Castle Rise. PL12 — 53 B4
Castle View. PL12 — 53 B4
Castlemead Clo. PL12 — 53 C2
Castlemead Dri. PL12 — 53 C2
Cedar Ct. PL12 — 53 E2
Channon Rd. PL12 — 53 B1
Chapel Rd. PL12 — 53 A2
Chapman Ct. PL12 — 53 A2
Chichester Cres. PL12 — 53 D3
Church Rd. PL12 — 53 C3
Churchill Walk. PL12 — 53 D4
Churchtown Vale. PL12 — 53 B3
Clear View. PL12 — 53 C2
Convent Clo. PL12 — 53 D2
Cook Ct. PL12 — 53 A2
Coombe Park. PL12 — 53 E3
Coombe Rd. PL12 — 53 E3
Courtlands. PL12 — 53 C4
Cowdray Clo. PL12 — 53 D3
Culver Rd. PL12 — 53 E3
Dane Ct. PL12 — 53 E3
Daws Ct. PL12 — 53 E3
Deacon Clo. PL12 — 53 E4
Deacon Dri. PL12 — 53 E4
Deer Park. PL12 — 53 D2
Down Clo. PL12 — 53 B3
Drakefield Dri. PL12 — 53 E2
Dunheved Rd. PL12 — 53 D3
Edwards Cres. PL12 — 53 A3
Elliott Clo. PL12 — 53 C3
Ellwell Rd. PL12 — 53 E2
Essa Rd. PL12 — 53 D3
Fairmead Mews. PL12 — 53 A2
Fairmead Rd. PL12 — 53 B2
Fairway. PL12 — 53 B3
Farm La. PL12 — 53 B4
Fenten Pk. PL12 — 53 D2
Fernside Way. PL12 — 53 B2
Fore St. PL12 — 53 E3
Forge La. PL12 — 53 A1
Forsythia Dri. PL12 — 53 A2
Foxglove Way. PL12 — 53 A2
Frith Rd. PL12 — 53 C2
Frobisher Dri. PL12 — 53 D3
Gallacher Way. PL12 — 53 A2
Gilston Rd. PL12 — 53 B1
Glanville Ter. PL12 — 53 E1
Glebe Av. PL12 — 53 D2
Gordon Ct. PL12 — 53 B3
Greenfield Rd. PL12 — 53 B3
Grenfell Av. PL12 — 53 A2
Hallett Clo. PL12 — 53 A2
Hardings Clo. PL12 — 53 C1
Hawks Pk. PL12 — 53 A3
Hawthorns. PL12 — 53 A2
Hearl Rd. PL12 — 53 A2
Heritage Clo. PL12 — 53 D1
Hessary Vw. PL12 — 53 D1
Hewitt Clo. PL12 — 53 B3
Higher Port View. PL12 — 53 D3
Highfield Pk. PL12 — 53 A2
Hillside Av. PL12 — 53 E2
Hillside Rd. PL12 — 53 D2
Hobbs Cres. PL12 — 53 B3
Hodge Clo. PL12 — 53 B3
Holcroft Clo. PL12 — 53 C3
Home Park Rd. PL12 — 53 E2
Homer Pk. PL12 — 53 C2
Howard Clo. PL12 — 53 C2
INDUSTRIAL & RETAIL:
Gwel-Avon Business Pk. PL12 — 53 C1
Moorlands Trading Est. PL12 — 53 A1
Saltash Business Pk. PL12 — 53 A1
Saltash Ind Est. PL12 — 53 B1

Saltash Parkway
  Ind Est. PL12   53 A1
Jackson Way. PL12   53 D2
Jubilee Clo. PL12   53 C2
Kerswick Ct. PL12   53 C1
Killigrew Av. PL12   53 C4
King Edward Rd. PL12   53 D3
Lander Rd. PL12   53 E2
Langerwell Clo. PL12   53 A2
Langerwell La. PL12   53 A2
Larch Clo. PL12   53 A2
Leat View. PL12   53 A2
Linnet Clo. PL12   53 A3
Liskeard Rd. PL12   53 A1
Lollabury Rd. PL12   53 C2
Long Acre. PL12   53 A1
Long Park Rd. PL12   53 C3
Longmeadow Rd.
  PL12   53 D2
Longview Rd. PL12   53 C2
Love La. PL12   53 D3
Lower Fore St. PL12   53 E3
Lower Port View. PL12   53 D3
Lynher Dri. PL12   53 D4
Manor Park. PL12   53 B3
Marlborough Clo.
  PL12   53 D3
Maybrook Dri. PL12   53 B3
Meadowsweet Pk.
  PL12   53 A3
Meadway. PL12   53 C4
Middlefield Clo. PL12   53 A2
Montgomery Clo. PL12   53 C2
Moorland Vw. PL12   53 E1
Moorlands La. PL12   53 B1
Mortimore Clo. PL12   53 C2
Mote Park. PL12   53 A2
Mulberry Rd. PL12   53 C3
New Rd. PL12   53 B2
Newman Rd. PL12   53 E2
Nilch Pk. PL12   53 A2
North Rd. PL12   53 E2
Oaklands Dri. PL12   53 B2
Oaklands Grn. PL12   53 B2
Old Ferry Rd. PL12   53 E2
Parkesway. PL12   53 C3
Pill La. PL12   53 D1
Plougastel Dri. PL12   53 D2
Plough Green. PL12   53 A2
Ploughboy Mews.
  PL12   53 A2
Pollard Clo. PL12   53 A3
Pollards Way. PL12   53 C1
Pondfield Rd. PL12   53 A2
Porter Way. PL12   53 B2
Pounds Park. PL12   53 E2
Prospect La. PL12   53 A2
Prospect Walk. PL12   53 A2
Rashleigh Alley. PL12   53 C4
Ridgeway. PL12   53 C4
River View. PL12   53 E1
Rowan Ct. PL12   53 A3
Russell Clo. PL12   53 B2
Rye Hill. PL12   53 A3
St Andrews Clo. PL12   53 B3
St Annes Rd. PL12   53 C2
St Georges Rd. PL12   53 C2
St Stephens Hill. PL12   53 B4
St Stephens Rd. PL12   53 C3
Saltash By-Pass. PL12   53 A1
Saltmill La. PL12   53 D1
Sandquay La. PL12   53 E2
Sleep Clo. PL12   53 A2
Smithfield Dri. PL12   53 A2
Smiths Way. PL12   53 A2
Smithys Clo. PL12   53 B1
Snell Dri. PL12   53 B1
Southfield. PL12.   53 B2
Spencer Gdns. PL12   53 D3
Spire Hill Pk. PL12   53 B3
Stanlake Clo. PL12   53 C3
Station Rd. PL12   53 E3
Summerfields. PL12   53 B4
Sunningdale Rd. PL12   53 B3
Sycamore Rd. PL12   53 A2
Tamar Bridge. PL12   53 F3
Tamar St. PL12   53 F3
Tamar Vw. PL12   53 E4
Tannery Ct. PL12   53 B3
Tavy Rd. PL12   53 E2
Taylor Clo. PL12   53 B2
Taylor Rd. PL12   53 B1
The Bridges. PL12   53 D4
The Brook. PL12   53 C1
The Close. PL12   53 A2

The Court. PL12   53 A3
The Green. PL12   53 A2
*The Hedgerows,
  Sycamore Rd. PL12   53 A2
The Keep. PL12   53 A2
The Rivers. PL12   53 D4
The Speares. PL12   53 A3
The Square. PL12   53 A2
Thorn La. PL12   53 B2
Tincombe Rd. PL12   53 B3
Tobruk Rd. PL12   53 C2
Torbridge Clo. PL12   53 B2
Tower Ct. PL12   53 A3
Tower View. PL12   53 C4
Trelawney Rd. PL12   53 D3
Two Hills Pk. PL12   53 A3
Uplands. PL12   53 C4
Valley Rd. PL12   53 D3
Victoria Rd. PL12   53 E3
Vincent Way. PL12   53 E3
Warfelton Cres. PL12   53 C3
Warfelton Gdns. PL12   53 C3
Warraton Clo. PL12   53 C2
Warraton Rd. PL12   53 C2
Wentworth Rd. PL12   53 B3
Wesley Rd. PL12   53 E3
Westbourne Ter. PL12   53 E2
Willow Grn. PL12   53 B3
Windmill Hill. PL12   53 D3
Windsor La. PL12   53 D3
Wood Acre. PL12   53 A1
Wood Clo. PL12   53 A2
Yellowtor Ct. PL12   53 A3
Yellowtor Rd. PL12   53 A3

TINTAGEL

Atlantic Rd. PL34   27 B4
Atlantic Way. PL34   27 B5
Back Land. PL34   27 C4
Bossiney Rd. PL34   27 B6
Castle View. PL34   27 A5
Church Hill. PL34   27 A6
Danmore Clo. PL34   27 B6
Fore St. PL34   27 B5
Fosters La. PL34   27 B6
Gavercoombe Pk. PL34   27 B5
King Arthurs Ter. PL34   27 B5
Knights Clo. PL34   27 B5
Laura Clo. PL34   27 C5
Merlins Way. PL34   27 D6
Molesworth La. PL34   27 C6
Rounds La. PL34   27 C6
Trenale La. PL34   27 D6
Vicarage Hill. PL34   27 B6
Westground Way. PL34   27 D5

TORPOINT

Adams Clo. PL11   54 C3
Adams Cres. PL11   54 C3
Adela Rd. PL11   55 F3
Albion Bungalows.
  PL11   55 G3
Albion Ct. PL11   55 G3
Albion Rd. PL11   55 G3
Alexandra Ter. PL11   55 G5
Antony Rd. PL11   55 C1
*Arthur Ter,
  Bellvue Sq. PL11   55 H4
Barossa Rd. PL11   55 H4
Beech Clo. PL11   55 E4
Bellevue Sq. PL11   55 H4
Bickern Rd. PL11   55 G3
Borough La. PL11   54 C2
Borough Pk. PL11   54 B2
Buller Clo. PL11   55 F4
Buller Rd. PL11   55 F3
Carbeile Rd. PL11   55 E3
Carew Ter. PL11   55 H4
Carlyon Clo. PL11   54 D2
Cedar Clo. PL11   54 D4
Cedar Dri. PL11   54 D4
Chapel Row. PL11   55 H4
Chapeldown Rd. PL11   54 D4
Chestnut Clo. PL11   55 E4
Clarence Rd. PL11   55 F3
Clegg Av. PL11   54 C3
Colwyn Rd. PL11   55 F4

Cremyll Rd. PL11   55 G5
Davy Clo. PL11   54 D3
Elliot Sq. PL11   55 H4
Ferry St. PL11   55 H4
Fisgard Way. PL11   54 A3
Fistral Clo. PL11   54 D2
Fore St. PL11   55 H3
Frobisher Way. PL11   54 B3
Goad Av. PL11   54 B3
Goad Clo. PL11   54 D3
Gordon Ter. PL11   55 F5
Gravesend Gdns. PL11   55 G3
Grove Pk. PL11   54 B3
Gurney Clo. PL11   54 D3
Gwithian Clo. PL11   54 D2
Hamoaze Rd. PL11   55 G5
Harbour St. PL11   55 H3
Harvey St. PL11   55 H3
Hawthorn Av. PL11   54 D4
Ince Clo. PL11   54 D2
INDUSTRIAL & RETAIL:
  Trevol Business Pk.
    PL11   54 A3
Jago Av. PL11   55 F4
Kempton Ter. PL11   55 G4
Kernow Clo. PL11   54 C3
Khyber Clo. PL11   55 F3
King St. PL11   55 H4
Kingsley Av. PL11   55 F5
Kynance Clo. PL11   54 D2
Lamorna Rd. PL11   54 B2
Langdon Down Way.
  PL11   54 C3
Liscawn Ter. PL11   55 G4
Macey St. PL11   55 H4
Maker Rd. PL11   55 F4
Maple Av. PL11   55 E4
Marine Ct. PL11   55 G5
Marine Dri. PL11   55 G5
Mill La. PL11   55 E4
Millhouse Pk. PL11   55 E4
Moorview. PL11   55 G3
Mount Edgcumbe Ter.
  PL11   55 G5
Murdoch Rd. PL11   54 C3
Navy Ter. PL11   55 H5
Nelson St. PL11   55 G4
North Rd. PL11 .   55 G4
Park Rd. PL11   55 G4
Peacock Av. PL11   54 C4
Pencair Av. PL11   54 C4
Pendennis Clo. PL11   54 D3
Pendilly Av. PL11   54 D4
Pengelly Hill. PL11   55 E1
Penlee Pk. PL11   54 C2
Pentire Rd. PL11   54 D2
Primrose Clo. PL11   54 D4
Quarry St. PL11   55 H3
Roberts Av. PL11   55 F4
Roeselare Av. PL11   55 F3
Roeselare Clo. PL11   55 F4
Rowe St. PL11   55 H4
St James Rd. PL11   55 G4
Salamanca St. PL11   55 G4
Sango Rd. PL11   55 F5
Sconner Rd. PL11   55 F3
Sennen Clo. PL11   54 D2
Sycamore Dri. PL11   55 E4
Sydney Rd. PL11   55 F3
Talbot Way. PL11   54 A3
Tamar St. PL11   55 H4
Thankes Clo. PL11   55 F2
Thanckes Dri. PL11   55 F2
The Lawns. PL11   55 F3
The Meadows. PL11   54 C2
The Mews. PL11   54 D4
Tregoning Rd. PL11   54 D4
Trelawney Clo. PL11   54 C3
Trelawney Rise. PL11   54 C3
Trematon Clo. PL11   54 D4
Trengrouse Av. PL11   54 D4
Trevol Rd. PL11   54 B3
Trevett View. PL11   54 C2
Trevithick Av. PL11   54 C2
Trevol Pl. PL11   54 A4
Trevol Rd. PL11   54 A4
Trevorder Clo. PL11   54 D5
Trevorder Rd. PL11   54 D4
Vicarage Rd. PL11   55 G4
Victoria St. PL11   55 G4
Wavish Pk. PL11   54 C3
Well Park Rd. PL11   55 F3
Wellington St. PL11   55 H4
Westlake Clo. PL11   55 E3
Windsor Ter. PL11   55 H3
Woodland Way. PL11   55 E3

York Rd. PL11   55 G3

TRURO

*Adelaide Ter,
  Crescent Rd. TR1   57 E4
Agar Ct. TR1   57 G4
Agar Rd. TR1   57 G4
Albert Pl. TR1   57 E5
Albert St. TR1   56 C4
Alma Rd. TR1   56 C4
Alverton Ct. TR1   57 G3
Alverton Ter. TR1   57 G3
Arch Hill. TR1   57 E6
Arundell Pl. TR1   57 F5
Ashley Rd. TR1   57 E5
Avondale Rd. TR1   56 D4
Back Quay. TR1   57 F4
Barrack La. TR1   57 F5
Barton Meadow. TR1   56 D3
Bedruthan Av. TR1   57 G2
Beechwood Gdns. TR1   57 H2
Behenna Dri. TR1   56 B4
Benson Rd. TR1   57 E3
Bishop Temple Rd.
  TR1   57 H3
Bishops Clo. TR1   57 F2
Blackberry Way. TR1   57 H3
Bodmin Rd. TR1   57 G2
Boscawen St. TR1   57 F4
Bosvean Gdns. TR1   56 D4
Bosvigo La. TR1   56 D4
Bosvigo Rd. TR1   57 E4
Brewers Rd. TR1   57 H3
Broad St. TR1   57 G3
Burley Clo. TR1   57 F5
Calenick St. TR1   57 F4
Campfield Hill. TR1   57 F4
Carclew St. TR1   57 F5
Carew Pole Clo. TR1   57 G5
Carew Rd. TR1   57 E3
Carey Park. TR1   57 E5
Carlyon Rd. TR1   57 F3
Carrine Rd. TR1   56 A5
Carvoza Rd. TR1   57 F3
Castle Rise. TR1   57 E3
Castle St. TR1   57 F4
Cathedral La. TR1   57 F4
Cathedral Vw. TR1   57 E2
Chainwalk Dri. TR1   57 E3
Chapel Hill. TR1   56 D5
Chapel Pl. TR1   57 F4
Chapel Row. TR1   57 F5
Charles St. TR1   57 F4
Chellew Rd. TR1   57 H3
Chirgwin Rd. TR1   57 G4
Chy Hwel. TR1   57 H3
City Rd. TR1   57 E4
*Claremont Ter,
  Castle Hope. TR1   57 E3
Cleswyth. TR1   56 C4
Coldrose Ct. TR1   56 D5
Comprigney Clo. TR1   56 D3
Comprigney Hill. TR1   56 D3
Coombes La. TR1   57 F4
Coosebean La. TR1   56 C3
Copes Gdns. TR1   57 E3
Cornish Cres. TR1   56 B4
Cornubia Clo. TR1   57 H2
Cotsland Rd. TR1   57 H3
Courtney Rd. TR1   57 E3
Crescent Gdns. TR1   56 D4
Crescent Rise. TR1   56 D4
Crescent Rd. TR1   57 E4
Cryon View. TR1   56 A4
Cyril Rd. TR1   57 E5
Daniell Ct. TR1   57 E5
Daniell Rd. TR1   57 E5
Daniell St. TR1   57 E5
Daubuz Clo. TR1   57 F2
Daubuz Ct. TR1   57 F3
David Penhaligon Way.
  TR1   57 F5
*Dereham,
  Chapel Hill. TR1   57 E4
Dobbs La. TR1   56 D4
Dudman Rd. TR1   56 C4
Duke St. TR1   57 F4
Eastland Clo. TR1   57 H4
Edward St. TR1   57 E4
Eliot Rd. TR1   57 E3
Elm Ct. TR1   57 F3

Elm Ct Gdns. TR1   57 F3
Enys Clo. TR1   57 E3
Enys Rd. TR1   57 E3
Epworth Clo. TR1   57 G2
Evea Clo. TR1   56 A5
Fairmantle St. TR1   57 F4
Falmouth Rd. TR1   57 E5
Ferris Town. TR1   57 E4
Frances St. TR1   57 E4
*Furniss Clo,
  St Austell St. TR1   57 G4
Galland Rd. TR1   56 C4
Gas Hill. TR1   57 G4
George St. TR1   57 E4
Gloweth Vw. TR1   56 A4
Green Clo. TR1   57 E6
Green La. TR1   57 E6
Green St. TR1   57 F4
Greenwith Clo. TR1   57 E5
Gregor Rd. TR1   57 H3
Grenville Rd. TR1   57 F4
Gwarnick Rd. TR1   57 F2
Gwendroc Clo. TR1   57 F5
Halwyn Pl. TR1   57 F2
Harbour Vw. TR1   57 H4
Harcourt Clo. TR1   56 C4
*Harrison Ter,
  The Crescent. TR1   56 D4
Harvey Rd. TR1   57 G3
Hendra Barton. TR1   57 E3
Hendra La. TR1   57 E3
Hendra Rd. TR1   57 E3
Hendra Vean. TR1   57 E2
High Cross. TR1   57 F4
Higher Newham La.
  TR1   57 G5
Higher Redannick. TR1   57 E5
Higher Trehaverne.
  TR1   57 E3
Hightertown. TR1   56 B4
Hill Crest Av. TR1   56 D3
Hunkin Clo. TR1   57 F2
Hurland Rd. TR1   57 H4
Huthnance Clo. TR1   57 H3
Hyne Corfe Gdns. TR1   56 C4
INDUSTRIAL & RETAIL:
  Newham Ind Est.
    TR1   57 F6
  Treliske Ind Est. TR1   56 A4
Infirmary Hill. TR1   57 F4
James Pl. TR1   57 G4
John St. TR1   57 E4
Kenna Park. TR1   56 B4
Kenwyn Church Rd.
  TR1   57 E3
Kenwyn Clo. TR1   57 E3
Kenwyn Hill. TR1   56 D2
Kenwyn Rd. TR1   57 E3
Kenwyn St. TR1   57 E4
Kerley Gro. TR1   56 B5
Kerris Gro. TR1   56 D5
Kestle Dri. TR1   56 C4
King St. TR1   57 F4
Kirby Rd. TR1   56 C4
Knights Hill. TR1   57 E3
Knoll Pk. TR1   57 H4
Lamellyn Dri. TR1   56 A4
Lemon Mews. TR1   57 F4
Lemon Quay. TR1   57 F4
Lemon St. TR1   57 F4
Lighterage Hill. TR1   57 G4
Little Castle St. TR1   57 F4
Lodge Dri. TR1   57 H4
Lower Redannick. TR1   57 E5
Lower Comprigney.
  TR1   56 D3
Lukes Clo. TR1   57 H4
Lychgate Dri. TR1   57 E3
Malabar Rd. TR1   56 B4
Malpas Rd. TR1   57 G4
Manor Gdns. TR1   57 G4
Meadow La. TR1   57 F5
Merrick Av. TR1   57 G2
Merrifield Clo. TR1   57 E5
Midway Dri. TR1   57 G2
Mill Race Pth. TR1   57 G5
Mitchell Hill. TR1   57 E4
Monterey Gdns. TR1   57 G2
Moresk Clo. TR1   57 F3
Moresk Gdns. TR1   57 F3
Moresk Rd. TR1   57 F3
Morlaix Av. TR1   57 E5
Murdoch Clo. TR1   57 G2
Nancemere Rd. TR1   57 G3
Nansavallon Rd. TR1   57 E6